lonely planet

POCKET ALGARVE

Daniel James Clarke

Contents

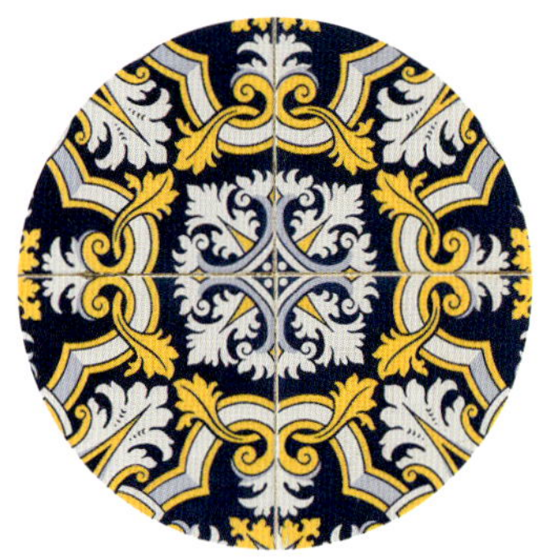

Top: *Azulejos* (glazed tiles), Loulé (p72)
Bottom: Street in Faro (p35)

Plan Your Trip 4

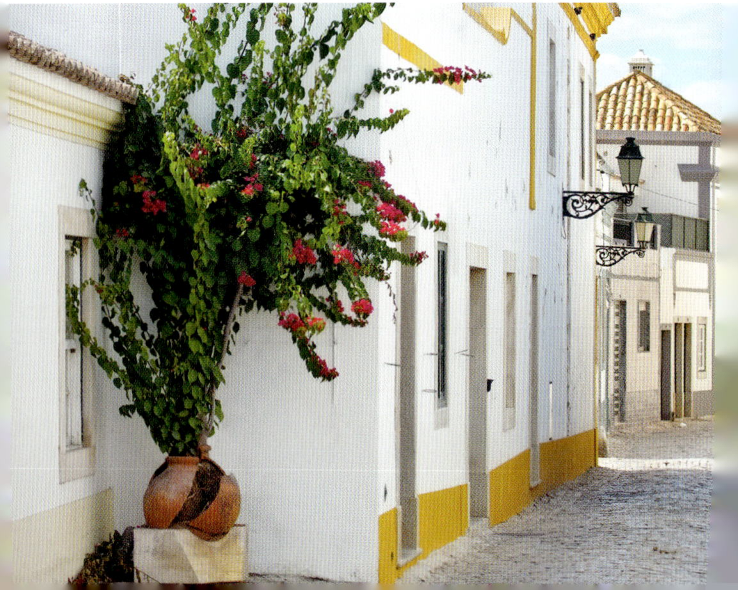

Explore Algarve 33

Algarve Toolkit 159

FROM TOP LEFT: ANDREI NEKRASSOV/SHUTTERSTOCK ©, ANIAD/SHUTTERSTOCK ©

★ Top Experiences

Worth a Trip

The Journey Begins Here

Portugal's southern, sun-kissed coastal playground earned summer stardom thanks to its sensational scalloped bays, craggy coves and idyllic islets. But the Algarve I adore isn't solely seaside or seasonal. Head inland, and you'll find a hushed hinterland of tranquil trails weaving together perennial villages, meet the new wave of vintners revitalising wineries, and encounter a revived pride in ancestral handicrafts and cultural celebrations. Unfurling across it all are the legacies of Moorish Al-Gharb, which gave the region its name. Beeline to those boundless beautiful beaches, but save time for the age-old Algarve awaiting around every detour-worthy corner.

Daniel James Clarke

@danflyingsolo

Daniel is a British-born travel writer who decided to make the Algarve home in 2018 after a lifetime of holidaying here.

Praia dos Estudantes (p136)

THE BEST

Coastal Experiences

Whether you're seeking sweeping golden sands, idyllic islets, cliff-backed craggy coves or surf-pounded shores, the Algarve's coastline abounds with paradisiacal *praias* (beaches). Lapped by the Atlantic Ocean, it's also ripe for aquatic adventures.

Island-hop around the **Parque Natural da Ria Formosa**, savouring local oysters and spotting flamingos. (p50)

Hike the spectacular **Percurso dos Sete Vales Suspensos**, stringing together cliff-flanked bays, photogenic rock formations, and the skylight-illuminated Benagil Cave. (p104; pictured above left)

Catch a wave on the **Costa Vicentina**, the west coast's rugged natural park renowned for its serious surf. (p152; pictured above right)

Scuba dive at Albufeira's **EDP Art Reef**, a gallery and artificial reef crafted from a decommissioned power plant. (p94)

Kayak between soaring sea stacks and pocket-sized bays at **Ponta da Piedade**, Lagos' dramatic headland. (p132)

Contemplate the call of the Atlantic Ocean at wind-ravaged **Cabo de São Vicente**, mainland Europe's southwesternmost point. (p148)

Right: Praia do Camilo (p136)

THE BEST

Food & Drink Experiences

Hand-harvested *conquilhas* (small clams), seafood steamed in traditional copper pans, and age-old recipes from former fishing villages keep the Algarve's menu mainly fish-focused. Pair with the region's revitalised wines and sweet treats.

Take a farm **cooking class** overlooking Tavira to learn how to cook with a *cataplana*, the region's signature clam-shaped cooking pot. (p62)

Sip wines amongst the vines at one of **Silves' bucolic wineries**, perfectly paired with sunset sessions or river sailings. (p120)

Devour a plate of charcoal-grilled **chicken piri-piri**, the Algarve's spicy speciality, in Guia. (p96)

Learn how to make typical Algarvian sweets, such as *doce fino* (colourful, fruit-shaped almond treats) at **Docaria do Sul**. (p124; pictured above right)

Board a fishing-boat tour to witness clams picked by hand and sample **Ilha da Culatra's oysters** straight from the estuary. (p53)

Harvest *fleur de sel* (sea salt) with an ancestral wooden net at net at the Spain-facing *salinas* (salt pans) in **Salmarim**. (p70)

Right: Traditional *cataplana* (cooking pot)

THE BEST

Outdoor Experiences

Golf may be the Algarve's most famed game. But with nearly year-round sunshine, three mountain ranges, and abundant offbeat trails, the region's often overlooked interior offers adrenaline-fuelled adventures and easy-going ambles.

Hike a stretch of the long-distance, interior-crossing Via Algarviana to **Fóia**, the region's highest peak. (p118; pictured above left)

Get a bird's-eye view of the Parque Natural do Sudoeste Alentejano e Costa Vicentina on a **tandem paraglide** with a pro. (p153)

Amble along the Roman road at **São Brás de Alportel** before jumping on a quad and bouncing across the cork-coated countryside. (p78)

Trace inland history on the **Masmorra Trail**, linking remote Mealha with the Anta da Masmorra dolmen. (p77)

Embark on a multiday trek along the **Rota Vicentina's Historical Way** in spring for a wildflower-carpeted wander between perennial villages. (p146)

Drive, hike or **sail upstream to Alcoutim** along the international border-defining Rio Guadiana. (p68)

Right: Rota Vicentina (p146)

FROM LEFT: EUNIKASOPOTNICKA/ISTOCKPHOTO/GETTY IMAGES ©,TLF IMAGES/SHUTTERSTOCK ©, TRABANTOS/SHUTTERSTOCK ©

THE BEST

Museum Experiences

Learn the Algarve's history while flitting between fossilised dinosaur footprints, dolmens and menhirs, Roman ruins, fortresses and sardine-dedicated spaces. Even the smallest villages have museums, proudly sharing regional heritage.

Wander Faro's walled **Vila Adentro**, the region's history recounted in Sé, the city's spectacular cathedral, and the Municipal Museum. (p37; pictured above left)

Understand Portugal's sardine obsession at the informative **Museu de Portimão**. (p108; pictured above right)

Tour the **Vila de Bispo Museum** to learn the area's prehistory before driving to nearby menhirs and fossilised Early Cretaceous footprints. (p154)

Visit Tavira's impressive **concert-hosting churches** to hear the history of fado, Portugal's soulful musical genre. (p58)

Learn about Portugal's Age of Discovery and its role in the slave trade at **Fortaleza de Sagres**' interpretation centre. (p148)

Stroll the open-air **Roman ruins of Milreu**, once a lavish villa, to see well-preserved mosaics. (p46)

Right: Roman ruins of Milreu (p46)

THE BEST

Moorish History Experiences

For over 500 years, the Moors – originally hailing from North Africa – ruled Al-Gharb, leaving a legacy far greater than the region's Arabic name. Discover their cultural and architectural influences at fortifications, museums and festivals.

Walk the crenellated walls of well-preserved **Castelo de Silves** to survey the surroundings as Moorish kings and poets did centuries before. (p124)

Visit the excavated **Banhos Islâmicos de Loulé**, the only (known) example of Islamic baths in Portugal. (p82)

Descend into an 18m-deep Almohad cistern-well inside Silves' **Museu Municipal de Arqueologia**, which houses multiple Moorish artefacts. (p125; pictured above right)

Marvel at the 11th-century Tavira Vase, a figurine-adorned clay vessel, at the **Núcleo Museológico Islâmico**. (p62)

Climb Aljezur's steep, narrow streets to the 10th-century **castle** before driving to nearby, cliff-perched Ribat da Atalaia, a ruined Islamic fortress. (p155)

Experience August's **Feira Medieval**, when the *adhan* (call to prayer), souk-like streets, and costumed performers transport Silves back in time. (p126; pictured above left)

THE BEST

Arts & Crafts Experiences

Many of the Algarve's ancestral handicrafts and techniques are in danger of disappearing as more towns trade traditions for tourism. Support those surviving by visiting a studio, booking a workshop, or buying locally made souvenirs.

Witness ancestral techniques at Loulé's network of **craft workshops** and prebook a class to hammer a *cataplana* or weave a basket. (p166)

Paint your own *azulejo* in Ferragudo while learning the history of these hand-painted, glazed ceramic tiles adorning buildings nationwide. (p108)

Join a **pottery workshop** in the Costa Vicentina's verdant hinterlands. (p154)

Learn all about cork, one of Portugal's biggest exports, on a **factory tour**. (p79)

Shop for traditional ceramics at Porches' pair of renowned **pottery studios**. (p109)

See the Algarve's contemporary side on a **street art tour**, taking in Lagos' murals before joining a workshop at creative LAC. (p139)

Pottery, Loulé (p73)

THE BEST

Village Experiences

Beyond the resorts, local life still plays out around markets, inland communities cling to local celebrations, and once-abandoned whitewashed hamlets are being repurposed. See a slower, more enduring Algarve by going slightly offbeat.

Find fishers still unloading their catch in fetching **Ferragudo** before falling in love with the bougainvillaea-draped cobbled streets. (p108)

Explore Alte's orange-tree-scented scenery, *fontes* (streams) and waterfall before road-tripping around the **Serra do Caldeirão's rural villages**. (p80)

Enjoy lunch or stay overnight at **Aldeia da Pedralva**, a nearly-abandoned hamlet now reborn as a community-funded diffused hotel. (p155)

Settle in for shellfish and swirling sand views at **Cacela Velha**, a diminutive, cliff-topping cobbled village. (p65)

Meet the medronho-brewing locals in minuscule **Marmelete** and learn more about the Algarve's fiercely strong firewater. (p126)

Book a spa or relax around the whimsical mountain village of **Caldas de Monchique**, revered for its thermal springs since Roman times. (p118)

Caldas de Monchique (p118)

SOPOTNICKI/SHUTTERSTOCK ©

Best for Kids

Spend a day at **Slide & Splash**, a fun-for-all-ages waterpark in Lagoa with kid-friendly pools, more adventurous teen-entertaining slides, and scheduled performances. (p110)

Ride the waves on a rigid inflatable boat to try and **spot dolphins in the wild** on a marine-biologist-guided tour beyond Faro's barrier islands. (p41)

Paddle in the clear, calm, semi-sheltered waters of **Praia da Salema** before finding the fossilised dinosaur footprints on the beach's western end. (p151)

Trade sand castles for sculptures at **SandCity**, where global landmarks, TV characters and annually changing additions are modelled entirely out of the sand. (p110)

Walk the buggy-suited wooden boardwalk wrapped around **Lagoa dos Salgados**' freshwater wetlands in the hope of spotting flamingos and other birdlife from the viewing platforms. (p97)

Best for Free

Swim, sunbathe and soak up scenic views on award-winning beaches such as Lagoa's Praia da Marinha or Albufeira's sweeping **Praia da Falésia**. (p90)

Walk the west coast's **Pontal da Carrapateira Trail**, something of an open-air museum, to dune-ribboned sands, Islamic ruins and a teeny fishing settlement. (p153)

Visit Loule's beautiful **Mercado Municipal** and traditional workshops to see artisans at work and learn about the Algarve's heritage handicrafts without pressure to purchase. (p83)

Cross the suspension bridge of the 1km **Passadiços Barranco do Demo** wooden boardwalk before descending into the verdant valley with a picnic. (p118)

Strut around splashy Vilamoura Marina and visit the small but thoughtfully curated **Quarteira History Museum** to hear how the region has changed over 6000 years. (p87)

Three Perfect Itineraries

Bountiful beaches and compact, walkable cities make sunbathing and sightseeing seamless in one day. Stay flexible when planning, allowing time for occasional beach detours, shade-seeking lunches, or overrunning boat tours.

Dolphins

FROM LEFT: PETER LLEWELLYN/GETTY IMAGES ©, TANYA USTENKO/SHUTTERSTOCK ©,TRAVELVIEW/SHUTTERSTOCK ©, TONY MILLS/SHUTTERSTOCK ©

TWO DAYS

A Quick Break

DAY ONE

On a flying visit, don't stray far. Base yourself in **Faro** (pictured above; p35) for two days, combining culture and coast. Spend the morning ambling around the old town's **medieval walls** (p38), **monumental cathedral** (p37) and convent-housed **Museu Municipal** (p40). After lunch, visit **Estoi's palace and Roman ruins** (p46) or, on weekdays, arrange a wine tasting at **Vinhas de Nexe** (p42). For dinner, book a fado-performing restaurant.

DAY TWO

Start the day with a **dolphin-spotting trip** (p41) followed by a lazy afternoon sunbathing and swimming on practically deserted **Ilha Deserta** (p41). Return to Faro for a jazz-accompanied **sunset cocktail** (p45) before sharing a seafood ***cataplana*** (seafood stew; p41).

SEVEN DAYS

Car-Free Highlights

DAY TWO

After one day in **Faro** (left), take the train west to **Silves** (two nights; p115). Visit the **Moorish Castle** (p124) and archeological museum before an afternoon **winery tasting and tour** (p123) or **sweet-making workshop** (p124).

DAY THREE

Take an early bus or taxi to hike the cliff-topping, beach-hopping **Percurso dos Sete Vales Suspensos** (p104); an early start will allow for a (slightly) calmer **Benagil Cave** (p104) kayak visit. In the afternoon, amble around or learn *azulejo* (glazed tile) making in pretty **Ferragudo** (pictured above centre; p108).

DAY FOUR

Take a train to **Lagos** (two nights; p129). Explore the **old town's history** (p134) by day, track the boardwalk towards **Ponta da Piedade** (p132) before sunset, and savour seafood, craft beers and cocktails after dark.

DAY FIVE

Relax on Lagos' **cliff-hugged beaches** (p136), surf or kayak. In the afternoon, take the bus to **Sagres** (p143) and visit the foreboding **fortress** (p148) and **Cabo de São Vicente** (p148), mainland Europe's southwesternmost point.

DAY SIX

Ride the rails east to **Olhão** (p48), store your bags, and spend the morning strolling the traditional fishing neighbourhoods. Then, explore the salt pans, wetlands and idyllic barrier islands of the **Parque Natural da Ria Formosa** (pictured above right; p50).

DAY SEVEN

If you've time before departure, plan a morning in laid-back **Tavira** (p55) before returning to the airport.

FIVE DAYS

East & Inland Road Trip

DAY ONE

Drive directly from the airport to **Loulé** (p73; pictured above left). Grab pastries at the neo-Arabic **Mercado Municipal** (p83) before touring the town's network of **artisan workshops** (p76). After lunch, drive a loop around the interior's **rural villages** (p80).

DAY TWO

Spend the morning in **São Brás de Alportel** (p78) learning about the Algarve of old at the costume, cork or Roman road museums. Afterwards, detour the scenic, rural roads towards **Alcoutim** (p71), a slumbering, former smuggling frontier town facing Spain.

DAY THREE

After a quick kayak across to Spain, track the **Rio Guadiana** (p68) downstream, stopping at miniature museums, and the medieval fortress, salt pans and reconstructed Vila Real de Santo António in **Castro Marim** (p69). Follow the N125 to teeny, cliff-topping **Cacela Velha** (pictured above right; p65) for fresh oysters and an unforgettable low-tide panorama en route to **Tavira** (two nights; p55).

DAY FOUR

Head to the **market** (p61) for breakfast and grab a picnic for a beach morning on **Ilha de Tavira** (p63). Catch an afternoon **church-hosted fado concert** (p61), wander whitewashed streets, and end the day **cooking a *cataplana*** (fish stew; p62) on a working farm.

DAY FIVE

Visit **Monterosa Olive Oil** (p64) for a morning factory tour. After lunch, stop by **Estoi's Roman ruins** (p46) before returning the car to fly out, or spend a final car-free day in Faro.

FROM LEFT: RALF GEITHE/SHUTTERSTOCK ©, STU.DIO/SHUTTERSTOCK ©

If You Have More Time

Plan half a day learning all about sardine-obsessed **Portimão** (p108), the Algarve's second city. **Tour a working *conserveira*** (canning factory; p108), devour freshly grilled seasonal sardines, and visit the excellent and contemporary **sardine canning industry museum** (p108).

Spend a day in the region's loftiest mountain range, the **Serra de Monchique** (p118). Start at **Fóia** (p118), the Algarve's highest point, to take in far-reaching panoramas of the forested mountains and glistening ocean. Then, either strap on hiking boots to embark on the toughest stretch of the long-distance **Via Algarviana** (p82), or go easy on a driving tour **meeting mountain makers** (p80), visiting **firewater-distilling villagers** (p126), or relaxing amongst **thermal springs** (p118).

Lean into the laid-back lifestyle of the **Costa Vicentina** (p143) for a couple of days. Catch serious waves at a **surf camp** (p152); learn to paraglide; detour down dirt track roads to windswept, rugged and **secluded shorelines** (p153); or tackle part of the multiday **Rota Vicentina** (p146), arguably Portugal's most impressive coastal ramble.

Serra de Monichique (p118)

SERGE MILES/SHUTTERSTOCK ©

Get Prepared

BOOK AHEAD

Three months before
Book major international **beach festivals** (p24), Michelin restaurants like Vila Joya, and accommodation (earlier for summer/large villas).

One month before
Schedule any **craft workshops** or **cooking classes**, private boat trips, excursions or guides. Finalise car hire.

Two weeks before
Make reservations at popular restaurants, book **winery tours**, and discount intercity train or bus tickets if arriving via Lisbon.

Manners Matter

Avoid comparisons with Spain and learn some local words rather than hoping that Spanish is similar. A kiss on each cheek is the typical greeting between women, or a man and woman. Cover up when leaving the beach, remembering that 'resort towns' are locals' actual hometowns. Skip takeaway coffee; take a caffeinated pause instead. Avoid visiting churches during Sunday Mass. Pregnant women and young families are usually prioritised in queues.

Confirming Opening Hours

The Algarve is highly seasonal, with numerous family-run businesses. Some close for a month or longer over winter without updating online hours. Most restaurants have afternoon breaks, while many museums and attractions close for lunch, on weekends and Mondays. Plan any itineraries accordingly. Phone to confirm hours; emails are often unanswered by small businesses.

Things to Know

Money Always carry cash. Many small restaurants, museums, and transport options don't accept cards. Bank-operated multibancos (ATMs: MB locally) usually have lower fees than the now-prolific international machines.

Parking scams In car parks requiring payment (cash; some via app), fake 'attendants' occasionally operate, highlighting spaces or reselling used tickets. Signal a polite 'no' and take a different space.

Events Alongside visitalgarve.pt, use cultugarve.com and shotgun.live to find local cultural and music events.

Geography The coast is often called *sotavento* (leeward east) and *barlavento* (windward west). Inland, the *barrocal* is the flatter, mid-region and *serra* the mountain ranges. Faro District is the Algarve's formal name.

TIPPING

Tipping isn't mandatory or expected. Locals often leave a euro or two on the table to express gratitude in restaurants. The IVA percentage displayed at the bottom of bills is VAT (included in menu prices), not a service charge.

Restaurants
For good service

€1–2

Snack bars/ cafes
If table service

Taxis
Round up

Tour guides
Group/private

DAILY BUDGET

BUDGET: Less than €125

- Coastal hostel dorm bed: **€25–40**
- Chicken piri-piri with a beer: **€12**
- Return ferry to the islands: **€5**
- Local museum or attraction ticket: **€2**

MIDRANGE: €125–250

- Simple boutique hotel: **€80–160**
- Shared seafood *cataplana* (seafood stew) with wine: **€30** per person
- Daily car hire: **€30**
- Beach parasol and sun lounger rental: **€15**

TOP END: more than €250

- 4/5-star hotel or upscale villa: **€160–300+**
- Wine-paired tasting menu: **€90+**
- Dolphin-spotting boat trip: **€50**
- Creative workshop or cooking class: **€50–100**

BEACH PLANNING

Use **InfoPraia** (*infopraia.apambiente.pt; or app*) to search nearby local beaches, check facilities and water quality, and see occupancy rates at certain seasonal shores. **MEO** (*beachcam.meo.pt*) hosts some live beach cams.

When To Go

Anytime. The Algarve might be summer sun fun, but each season comes with a compelling calling, from surf to spring wildflowers and autumn's wine harvest.

The year starts slow, calm and affordable, with many resort businesses hibernating over January. February brightens with almond blossoms and carnivals. Come spring, wildflowers line welcoming hiking trails, humpback whales might be sighted, Easter celebrations await, and migratory birds depart.

Summer brings soaring temperatures, prices, festivals and crowds, though peaceful pockets of sand can always be found. Autumn arrives with hike-friendly climes, growing surf, the much-anticipated wine harvest and birdwatching festivals. Winter (usually) offers some of Europe's warmest weather, resort bargains and, perhaps, an al-fresco Christmas lunch.

The Main Events

February–April: Easter celebrations start with colourful carnival celebrations. Dates depend on Lent, but **Loulé Carnival** (p83) is the biggest bash. Easter Sunday is a more sombre affair, with Loulé's **Festa da Mãe Soberana** (p83) procession and São Bras de Alportel's **Festa das Tochas Floridas** (p84) particularly memorable.

June: To celebrate the start of summer, street and beach parties abound. The Algarve's biggest is Carvoeiro's Black & White Night when thousands flock to the beach for DJs, bands and pop-up bars. Loulé's Festival MED, and Praia da Rocha's mega festivals, including Afro Nation, begin.

August: Summer's spotlight is firmly on seafood, with lively

Algarve Weather

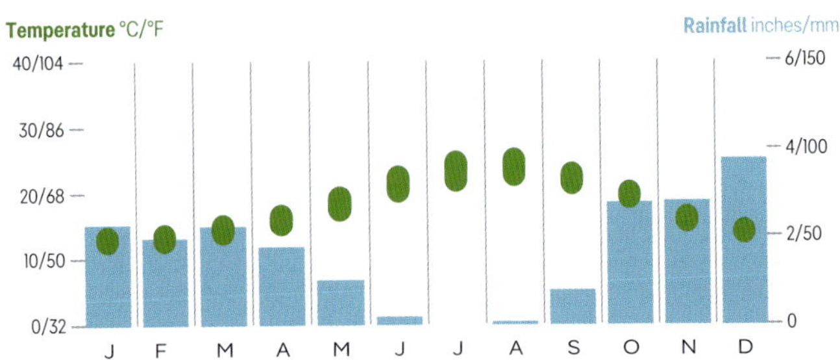

Loulé Carnival (p83)

gastronomic festivals accompanied by live music. **Olhão's Festival do Marisco** (p53) and **Portimão's Sardine Festival** (p111) are two of the biggest.

August: Step into Moorish history at Castro Marim's and Silves' **Medieval Fairs** (p126), with costumed reenactments, music, jousting and 'souks' hawking typical wares.

Local & Quirky Festivals

February: The village of Alta Mora awakens for its annual **Algarve Almond Blossom Festival** (p65), with pretty floral walks and a humongous almond pie. The region-wide Al-Mutamid Festival brings Arabic music back to the Algarve.

March or April: Otherwise peaceful Alcoutim hosts its smuggling-focused **Festival do Contrabando** (p71) every other year, complete with a floating, Spain-linking bridge, 'custom officers' and plenty of entertainment.

September: In late August, the **wine harvest** begins. Visit a winery for a day of picking, treading the traditional way by foot, and, of course, sampling the good stuff.

October: All eyes are on the west coast for a raft of events at the **Sagres Bird Watching Festival** (p152), followed by Aljezur's Sweet Potato Festival in November.

Seriously Seasonal Accommodation

Prices plummet in November, January and February, sometimes as much as 75% compared to July and August. Spring and autumn discounts are lesser, but arguably offer the best value versus experience. During UK school holidays in particular (summer, Easter and half-terms), prices rocket.

Getting There

Most European visitors (and limited North American flights) arrive via Faro's Gago Coutinho International Airport, renowned for long non-Schengen arrival queues during summer. Lisbon and Seville are alternative gateways.

From the Airport to Your Destination

By Taxi, Rideshare or Transfer

Taxis (exit, turn right) and rideshare apps, including Uber and Bolt (pickup near the bus stop), are plentiful, reaching downtown Faro in 15 minutes. Non-surge rideshares are usually cheaper (from around €5) as metered taxis charge for luggage.

To reach resorts further afield, prebookable private or shuttle-bus transfers are usually better value.

By Public Transport via Faro

Próximo's regular 16 bus (exit, turn left) takes 20 minutes to downtown Faro (€2.70, payable by cash or contactless onboard). From here, connect to regional buses or trains.

By Aerobus

Vamus' 56 Aerobus connects Faro Airport with Albufeira (€10, 40 minutes), Lagoa, Portimão (€13, 1¼ hours) and Lagos (€16, two hours) roughly every two hours in daylight (winter service is reduced).

Purchase tickets from the machine at the bus stop, online or in-app; the Vamus Tourist Pass includes a return journey. Map apps may recommend Rede Expressos; however, these services are for long-distance journeys, not within the Algarve.

From Alternative Airports

Lisbon

Regular Alfa Pendular and intercity trains (€23.55 walkup) link Lisbon and Faro in three to 3½ hours; change in Tunes for the western Algarve. If staying in Albufeira, Portimão or Lagos, Rede Expressos buses (rede-expressos.pt; prebook for discounts) are usually faster, more direct, and cheaper. Tickets include a complimentary Vamus bus connection.

Seville, Spain

Rede Expressos/Alsa and FlixBus operate a handful of daily bus connections from downtown Seville. It's two hours to Tavira (from €21 in advance) or five hours to Lagos. There is no Algarve–Spain railway.

Getting Around

The Algarve's affordable trains and regional Vamus bus network will take you between the south coast's main cities and resort towns. Inland, bus connections are less frequent, while all regional public transport is limited after dark. Renting a car allows much easier access to rural trails, villages and remote beaches.

Walking

In cities, downtown areas are relatively compact, making walking the best option for those able. Ample trails crisscross the interior mountains and coastal cliffs.

Train

CP Trains (cp.pt) are usually the fastest way to travel between destinations along the south coast, though some stations, such as Albufeira and Loulé, aren't within walking distance of the main tourist areas. Currently undergoing much-needed upgrades and electrification, the regional line is served by ageing, trundling carriages between Vila Real de Santo António (VRSA) and Lagos, sometimes requiring a change in Faro. Trains are elevated with stairs; few stations offer accessibility support. Strikes are scheduled periodically; check for notifications online.

Bus

Vamus (vamusalgarve.pt) operates the Algarve's integrated bus network, reaching most towns and villages. Inland services are

ULDISZILE/SHUTTERSTOCK ©

ESSENTIAL APP

Download the Vamus app to top up a scannable, prepaid QR code for bus discounts.

commuter-focused and often weekday-only. Evening services are sorely lacking across the region except within main cities, which have their own bus networks. Vamus' coaches are raised, limiting accessibility; city services usually have ramps. Avoid the higher-priced 56 Aerobus unless travelling to the airport.

Car

Hiring a car will allow you to explore fully and freely, especially around the interior and west coast. Surprisingly, few roads are coastal; the main region-crossing routes are the N125, with varying speed limits, and the A22 motorway (tolls are scheduled to end in 2025). GPS driving times are often optimistic inland, and coastal parking fills fast in summer. Park outside villages to avoid narrow streets, or on the edge of often-pedestrianised cities.

Taxi

Taxis and rideshares, including Uber and Bolt, are plentiful around popular beaches and coastal towns but are less readily available inland.

Cycling

New marked cycle paths, board-walks and cross-regional routes have recently seen cycling soar in popularity. Most large towns have at least one company offering road and e-bike rentals. Bikes can be transported on trains; Vamus buses usually only carry folded bikes in the luggage compartment.

Ferries & Boats

Regular, affordable, no-reservation ferries service most of the Ria Formosa's islands year-round, complemented by water taxis and boat tours.

Public Transport Essentials

Tourist Passes

CP's Algarve-only Tourist Travelcard costs (adult/child) €21.90/€15.90 for two days and €32.90/€23.90 for three days. Purchase at ticket offices.

The Vamus Tourist Pass, including the Aerobus, costs €35 for three days and €46 for seven days. Buy online or in the app. City bus networks have other pass options. Compare single and prepay prices before considering a pass.

Tickets & Prepaid Discounts

Trains and buses are single-class without peak fares or mandatory reservations (but rarely full). A return (*volta*) rather than a single (*ida*) doesn't offer savings.

Trains

At staffed stations, tickets must be bought before boarding. Elsewhere, buy with cash from the conductor onboard. Pay by card online or in CP's app; digital sales end 15 minutes before departure.

Buses

At the main bus stations (terminal *rodoviário*), purchase tickets from the desk when open; ticket machines are gradually being installed. Otherwise and elsewhere, use cash onboard. Some main route tickets are sold online. However, the easiest and most affordable option is prepayment (*pré-pago*) via the Vamus app, available in English. Create an account, add funds and, when boarding, state the destination and scan your QR code; savings can soon add up, with discounts of up to 40%. The app also works for the integrated local bus services (not Faro's Próximo).

ACCIDENTAL FARE EVASION

Paying onboard (cash only) regional trains is only allowed when boarding from unstaffed stations.

TICKETS

Prices are for full-price, non-prepaid tickets, with average timings in brackets.

	Train	Bus
Faro to Albufeira	€3.65 (35mins)	€5.80 (1¼hrs)
Faro to Portimão	€6.55 (1hr 25mins)	€6.90 (2hrs)
Faro to Lagos	€7.95 (1hr 50mins)	€6.90 (2½hrs)
Faro to VRSA	€5.65 (1hr 10mins)	€6.90 (1hr 55mins)

CITY BUS COMPANIES

*All prices are for one zone.

Faro (Próximo)
€1.30

Albufeira (Giro)
€2

Portimão (Vai e Vem)
€1.60

Lagos (Onda)
€1.20

A Few Surprises

Islamic influences, iconic chimneys, art in unusual places and unexpected donkey carts. The Algarve isn't all sun, sea and sand.

Unexpected 'Street' Art

An explosion of street art has illuminated the whitewashed Algarve in recent years. From painted electricity boxes and upcycled rubbish art by Portuguese Bordalo II in **Alcoutim** and **Praia de Faro** to Albufeira's **EDP Art Reef** underwater gallery, urban art abounds. Yet the country's original street art, the *calçada portuguesa*, still shines brightest. These patterned, polished black basalt and white limestone cobblestone pavements became prevalent during the **post-1755 earthquake** (p136) reconstruction. Find the prettiest examples in **Faro Baixa** (p39). Equally as dazzling are the *azulejos* (hand-painted, glazed, ceramic tiles). Arriving during the Moorish period, they became prevalent on walls and homes in the 16th century.

Chic Chimneys

The Algarve's distinctive chimneys (*chaminé* Algarvia) are often miscredited to the Moors. However, the ornamental, often elaborately patterned towers started appearing around the late 17th century. The more intricate the design, the longer its construction, and, importantly, the number of chimneys on each roof could communicate the residents' wealth. The villages of **Estoi** (p46) and **Porches** (p109) have well-preserved early examples.

Donkeys

Before joining the A22, blue signs warn who can't drive on motorways, including donkey carts. Donkeys were long part of the traditional farm workforce. Meet them on a **donkey-accompanied amble** (p154).

OFFBEAT ALGARVE

Cross the river border between Spain and Portugal by kayak, zipline or 'smuggling' bridge in **Alcoutim** (p71).

Find an unexpected **Buddha Stupa** (p81) with fluttering prayer flags in the remote Serra do Caldeirão.

Spot flamingos in the *salinas* (salt pans) around Olhão before floating in the **Mar Morto** (Dead Sea; p53).

Trade fado, Portugal's famed melancholic folk music, for the traditional Algarvian accordion, at the dedicated **museum** (p96).

MAURO RODRIGUES/SHUTTERSTOCK ©

Algarve chimney

PHOTORAPAGAO/SHUTTERSTOCK ©

Donkey

Explore Algarve

Worth a Trip

Algarve's Tours

Street in Faro (p35)
ANIAD/SHUTTERSTOCK ©

See p44
for eating, drinking and shopping listings

Explore Faro

Flourishing as Roman Ossónoba, remembered as the Moors' last stronghold, and conquered by King Alfonso III in 1249, Faro doesn't lack historical credentials. And that's not to mention the Phoenicians, plunderings, earthquakes or tsunami. Yet, without the west's more famous resorts, and devoid of beaches on its doorstep – though paradisiacal island-like sands are a short ferry away – most sun-seekers skipped the regional capital for decades. But in recent years, Faro has cemented its city-break credentials with creative cultural associations, elevated restaurants, marina-facing rooftop bars, urban vineyards, and renovated museums now complementing its majestic cathedral and pretty Cidade Velha (Old Town).

Getting Around

Walking

Faro's Old Town is mostly pedestrianised, flat and relatively compact, considering it's the regional capital.

Bus

Proximo, Faro's main bus company (with accessibility ramps), operates regular city services and connections to the beach (line 16, €2.70, cash or contactless onboard), also reachable by ferry. Proximo's terminus is alongside the main bus station, serving regional Vamus buses and long-distance coaches.

Train

Faro Train Station, near the bus terminal, is best for further-afield day trips to Olhão, Tavira or Lagos.

Faro
MARIAJUAREZ/SHUTTERSTOCK ©

THE BEST

MUSEUM Museu Municipal (p40)

MONUMENT Sé (p37)

BEACH ESCAPE Ilha Deserta (p41)

PERFORMANCE Fado na Igreja (p42)

BOAT TRIP Dolphin spotting (p41)

Faro (7km)
R Aboim Ascenção
R do Alportel
R General Teófilo da Trindade
R de Loulé
R Infante Dom Henrique
R da Atalaia
Igreja de Nossa Senhora do Carmo & Capela dos Ossos
Lg do Carmo
R Solto Mayor
R Cruz dos Mestres
Lg de São Pedro
R do Compromisso
Teatro Lethes
Lg do Estação
Train Station
R Francisco Barreto
R Teófilo Braga
R do Viola
R Gil Eanes
R do Forno
R de São Pedro
R Batista Lopes
R Lethes
R de Portugal
R da Barqueta
R Conselheiro de Bívar
R do Prior
R Filipe Alistão
R José Estêvão
Av da República
Pç Ferreira de Almeida
R Vasco da Gama
Museu Regional do Algarve
R 1 de Maio
Parque Natural da Ria Formosa
Pç Dom Francisco Gomes
R Dom F Gomes
R de Santo António
R Rebelo da Silva
Marina
Jardim Manuel Bívar
Igreja da Misericórdia
R Castilho
R Alexandre Herculano
Ocean Vibes
R da Misericórdia
R Rasquinho
CIDADE VELHA
R de São Francisco
R do Bocage
R Teresa Ramalho Ortigão
R Caçadores 4
Centro Ciência Viva do Algarve
Lg da Sé
Sé
R do Repouso
R Comandante Francisco Manuel
Faro Story Spot
R do Trem
Museu Municipal
Igreja de São Francisco
R do Castelo
Cais das Portas do Mar
Lg do Castelo
Ilha da Barreta
Restaurante O Castelo
R Nova do Castelo
Lg de São Francisco
Ilha da Culatra
For more see
Top Experiences p37
Experiences p40
Eating p44
Drinking p45
Shopping p45
0 200 m
0 0.1 miles

★ TOP EXPERIENCE

Sé, Faro's Cathedral

Faro's spectacular centrepiece, Sé (officially Igreja de Santa Maria), has seen its share of history. A Roman temple, and later a mosque, stood here before repairs and redesigns commenced in 1251, two years after the Christian Reconquista. Tickets include access to the church, museum, bell tower and bone chapel.

MAP: **C5**

Cathedral

Since its major 15th-century refurbishment, the cathedral has experienced, among other things, a devastating fire caused by an English attack and two earthquakes. The result is an interesting assembly of Renaissance, Gothic, mannerist and baroque styles. The magnificent 18th-century gilded altarpiece dazzles, but each of the dozen chapels, particularly the baroque Our Lady of Pleasure Chapel crafted from marble and stucco, impresses. A supplied pamphlet provides details on each. A ramp has been constructed to improve access, though the museum and tower are accessed via stairs.

Sacred Museum

From the first floor, dedicated to the Museu Capitular, enjoy a closer inspection of the early 18th-century organ before taking in the chapter rooms' sacred art, sculptures and chalices from the Algarve's Diocese collection.

Bell Tower & Chapel of Bones

It's a narrow but fairly brief climb up to the bell tower, which retains its original 13th-century base. Sweeping panoramas of the Vila Adentro and the Ria Formosa's islands await from the top. Before leaving, take a little time to explore the cloister, leading to a small chapel of bones and a temporary exhibition space.

PLANNING TIPS

Sé (*adult/concessions €5/€3.50*) is open year-round from 10am to 5.30pm Monday to Friday, and 9.30am to 3.30pm Saturday. Hours are extended in summer. Allow at least one hour.

Walk Faro's Cidade Velha

Faro's Cidade Velha (Old Town) contains three neighbourhoods. The walled Vila Adentro (Inside Village), the Mouraria (district for the expelled Moors), and to the west, the former Bairro Ribeirinho (Fishing Neighbourhood). Take them all in on this easy-going amble through the city's history.

START	END	LENGTH
Arco da Vila	Marina	3.6km; 1¼ hours

1 Grand Entrance

Start at the Vila Adentro's most impressive entrance, the **Arco da Vila**, an almost church-like, Italian-designed facade added in 1812 as part of the reconstruction post-earthquakes. See the Porta Árabe (Arabic Door) under the thick, Moorish-built archway.

2 Historic Square

Largo da Sé, a spacious orange tree-lined square flanked by history-weighted buildings is the Vila Adentro's nucleus. The centrepiece is **Sé**, Faro's cathedral, though the Paço Episcopal de Faro (*€2.50*) – the former bishop's palace, its library was looted by the Earl of Essex in 1597 – is worth visiting for its *azulejos*. Amble the pedestrianised streets towards the convent-housed **Museu Municipal**. A statue of King Afonso III, who oversaw the reconquest of the Algarve, stands in front.

3 Walk The Walls

Exit through **Arco do Repouso**, turning left to briefly see the baby blue **Palacete Belmarço**, a private residence, before returning to track the best-preserved section of the walls. A dilapidated beer factory, now the cultural association **Associação Recreativa e Cultural de Músicos**, stands where the Moorish castle once was. Follow the walls along the waterfront for scenic views of the **Ria Formosa** (p50).

4 Marina Square

Returning to the marina-facing **Praça Dom Francisco Gomes** and **Jardim Manuel Bivar**, admire the melange of architectural styles, including 16th-century **Igreja da Misericórdia** and 20th-century Banco de Portugal's neo-Moorish and mosaic features. The square regularly hosts an artisanal market.

5 Pretty Streets

Enter the old Mouraria, now *baixa* (downtown), and walk along **Rua de Santo António**, lined with stately homes turned shops and carpeted with some of the region's most impressive and colourful *calçadas* (cobblestone pavements). Find **Museu Regional do Algarve** at the end of the street before ambling onwards, passing **Teatro Lethes**.

6 Churches & Chills

Reaching **Largo do Carmo**, visit **Igreja de Nossa Senhora do Carmo** to see the haunting chapel of bones. If it's open, peek inside the more intimate Igreja de São Pedro.

7 Former Fishing Neighbourhood

Explore the cluster of streets in the former **Bairro Ribeirinho**, where dilapidated graffitied buildings sit alongside renovated homes. There are plenty of bars for a refreshing drink before returning to the marina.

EXPERIENCES

Admire Faro's Archaeological Finds

MUSEUM

MAP: 1 P36 C5

Housed in and around the cloisters of the former Convento de Nossa Senhora da Assunção, the architecture of the **Museu Municipal** (*cm-faro.pt; adult/concessions €2/€1*) is as impressive as its displays. Allow at least an hour to explore the predominantly Faro-focused collection, including religious paintings and Islamic artefacts. The Roman finds from **Milreu** (p46) are particularly impressive, with the mesmerising and well-preserved Mosaic of Oceanus stealing the spotlight. The convent was constructed in the former Jewish neighbourhood where the printing press was first introduced to Portugal in 1487 to print a Hebrew Bible. Following renovations to make the building accessible, it reopened in 2024 with new access ramps and a lift. The museum is closed on Mondays.

Study the Algarve's Heritage

MUSEUM

MAP: 2 P36 D3

The ethnographic **Museu Regional do Algarve** (*cm-faro.pt; €1.50*), closed on Sundays and Mondays, recalls the region's heritage across several spacious rooms. It's a mishmash of chronology, displaying exhibits on traditional economic practices, such as palm weaving, cork harvesting and embroidery, alongside recreations of typical regional family rooms, ancestral outfits, and fishing boats. While most text is in Portuguese (a translation app is helpful), it's a highly visual museum, displaying many aspects of ancestral Algarvian life that are barely visible along the coast nowadays.

Beeline to the Beach

BEACH

It takes a little effort to reach Faro's beaches, but the almost endless sands are the reward. The city's main beach, **Praia de Faro** (MAP: 3 P36 A1), has an island-like feeling, although it's a sandy peninsula. Accessible in 20 to 30 minutes by bus, road (there's parking across the bridge, but the main car park is before), or ferry from **Cais das Portas do Mar** (MAP: 4 P36 B5; *cm-faro.pt; adult/child from €2.30/€1.10 one-way*), the inhabited beach has plenty of bars, facilities and space to spread out – though flights landing nearby can disrupt the peace. The ferries don't offer step-free boarding, but buses have ramps, and the beach has an amphibious chair available at the seasonal lifeguard station.

Escape to a Deserted Island

ISLANDS

MAP: 5 P36 C6

Blissfully uninhabited and relatively wild, the only structure on Ilha da Barreta is the solar-powered, daytime-only restaurant, **Estaminé** (p45) , earning the island its second name, **Ilha Deserta** (deserted island). There's no need for a lunch reservation to visit; turn up (pack everything you need) and amble to an empty spot. The year-round ferries are operated by Animaris (*ilhadeserta.com; from €5*), who also run a hop-on hop-off service (*adult/child €17.50/€35*) to some of the other islands in the **Parque Natural da Ria Formosa** (p50). In summer, public ferries (*cm-faro.pt; adult/child from €3.50/€2 one-way*) operate to **Ilha da Culatra** (p51).

Stroll a Birdlife Boardwalk

WALKING TRAIL

Birdlife thrives on the lagoon side of Praia de Faro. Colourful long-beaked Eurasian hoopoe, flamingos and, on lucky occasions, the rare purple gallinule are just a few of the potential seasonal sightings along the **Passadicos de Loule** (MAP: 6 P36 **A1**; *passadicosloule litoral.pt*) boardwalk, a 4.9km, low-intensity linear trail beginning in Vale de Lobo, but joinable from the **Quinta do Lago** (see 6) resort, or via the dirt track Ludo Trail extension (enter near Praia de Faro's large car). To create a circular route, returning via the beach, cross at the Quinta do Lago bridge.

Spot Cetaceans in the Wild

BOAT TRIP

MAP: 7 P36 **B4**

Dolphin pods play in the deep blue beyond the Ria Formosa's barrier islands, and, increasingly in recent years, orcas and whales are sighted. Multiple boats depart the marina seeking cetaceans, with marine biologist-led **Ocean Vibes** (*oceanvibesalgarve.com; €50*) one of the most conscious operators. Over three hours, you'll ride the waves on a RIB (rigid inflatable boat) in the hope of spotting marine mammals. While sightings are never guaranteed, chances are high

THE CATAPLANA

The *cataplana* (seafood stew) is the Algarve's most distinctive dish. However, the standalone word refers to the clam-like, airtight cooking pot used to slowly steam various recipes, mainly with a tomato, onion, pepper and herb base. *Cataplana de marisco* (seafood), usually served to share, is the most prevalent. While historical records are lacking, it's believed the Moors introduced the signature utensil due to its cooking method's similarities with Morocco's tagine. The most illustrious cataplanas are hand-crafted from copper, though modern versions are lined with tin or stainless steel to avoid toxins. Expect to wait at least 30 minutes for a fresh *cataplana*.

year-round, with the particular species (common, striped or bottlenose dolphins) depending on the season. March and April are best for migrating whales, while August might bring hammerhead sharks. A handful of other operators around the marina offer alternative boat tours, including to the Ria Formosa.

Sip Wines Amongst the Vines VINEYARD

MAP: 8 P36 C1

Growing grapevines on Faro's fringes, **Vinhas de Nexe** (*vinhasdenexe.com; from €28*) is only a 15-minute taxi ride from the centre. First bottled in 2022, the vineyard (production is off-site) is one of the Algarve's youngest, and Mónica's 90-minute tours will guide you through the vines before a tapas-paired wine tasting of their blends, including Portugal's prime grape, Touriga Nacional. Private weekday visits require booking at least 48 hours in advance.

See Spooky & Serene Sacred Spaces CHURCHES

Faro isn't short of historic places of worship, although with variable hours, peering inside is down to well-timed luck. The twin-tower-fronted, 18th-century **Igreja de Nossa Senhora do Carmo** (MAP: 9 P36 C2; €2) holds regular visiting hours, excluding Sunday Mass. Inside, the gilded decor is mesmerising, yet it's the creepy Capela dos Ossos, its walls embedded with over 1000 exhumed skulls and bones of Carmelite monks, that leaves lasting memories. Also worth visiting is the **Igreja de São Francisco** (MAP: 10 P36 D5) for its impressive interior gilding and blue-and-white *azulejos* narrating the life of Saint Francis.

Fall in Love with Fado CONCERTS

Fado, Portugal's melancholic guitar-accompanied musical genre hails from the working-class neighbourhoods of Lisbon, the country's capital. It can be appreciated at **Fado na Igreja's** (*facebook.com/*

GOLF & THE GOLDEN TRIANGLE

The expanse of luxury hotels, villas, golf courses, and fine dining west of Faro is collectively called the Golden Triangle. It includes the two closest resorts of Quinta do Lago and Vale do Lobo, Portugal's largest marina in the resort of Vilamoura (p96), and the inland town of Almancil, known for its clutch of accoladed restaurants. While much of the land is resort-owned, the beaches, restaurants and most roads are publicly accessible. With a dozen esteemed golf courses and academies (some with PGA pros) around the Golden Triangle, it's a terrific place to tee-off or improve your game.

fadonaigreja; from €10) one-hour, Wednesday to Friday afternoon concerts inside the reconstructed 16th-century **Igreja da Misericórdia** (MAP: 11 P36 **C4**). The Museu Municipal hosts periodic performances within its cloisters, as does **Restaurante O Castelo** (MAP: 12 P36 **C5**). Guitar recitals are also regularly performed inside the city walls, accessed via the tourism office's staircase; ask for current schedules and tickets.

Watch a Football Match SPORT

MAP: 13 P36

Football is as much part of Portuguese soul as fado, and with the **Estádio Algarve** (*estadioalgarve.pt*), on the city's fringes, there's the occasional game to be seen. Constructed for the 2004 UEFA Euros, it's the region's largest stadium, although Lisbon and the north tend to host any major games.

Tour (or See a Show) at Teatro Lethes THEATRE

MAP: 17 P36 **D2**

Faro's former 17th-century Jesuit college turned theatre, **Teatro Lethes** (*teatrolethes.com; adult/child €5/€3*), is the city's most elegant cultural venue. With plush burgundy seats, four wooden tiered terraces and a *trompe l'oeil* ceiling, it's worth checking the intimate venue's programme before your arrival. Twice a month, guided tours allow for a better appreciation, including the backstage areas.

BEST FOR KIDS

Jardim da Alameda João de Deus

MAP: 14 P36 **D5**

This leafy, semi-enclosed park has free-roaming peacocks, a playground, mini golf and a neo-Moorish facade fronting the city's library.

Centro Ciência Viva do Algarve

MAP: 15 P36 **B5**

Entertain the little ones at the city's science museum covering coastal ecosystems in and beyond the Ria Formosa (*adult/child €5/€3*).

Faro Story Spot

MAP: 16 P36 **C5**

Although slightly overpriced, kids will appreciate this multimedia museum covering Faro and the Ria Formosa in a 35-minute immersive experience (*farostoryspot.pt; adult/child €13/€7*).

Join the City's Celebrations EVENTS

Faro has a busy annual schedule (*cm-faro.pt/pt/agenda*). Two of the largest summer festivals are the 11-day, seafood-celebrating **Festa da Ria Formosa** in July and August, and August's **Folkfaro**, the region's largest folklore event, spotlighting many otherwise overlooked traditions and dances. In October, the centuries-old **Feira De Santa Iría** is fun for all ages.

LISTINGS

Best Places for...

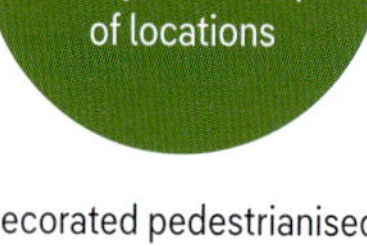
See p36 for map of locations

❸ Budget ❸❸ Midrange ❸❸❸ Top End

Eating

Local Favourites

Pastelaria Coelho ❸

18 D4

Friendly snack bar with a rear terrace serving breakfast, snacks, cakes, lunch specials and traditional dinners. *7.30am-midnight Sun-Fri*

O Recife ❸

19 C2

Churrasqueira (grill restaurant) and takeaway serving chicken piri-piri by the half or whole. *noon-3pm & 7-10pm Thu-Tue*

Vó Bela ❸

20 D1

Family-run restaurant specialising in *petiscos* (small plates), seafood and harder-to-find Portuguese recipes. *noon-3pm Tue-Sun & 7-10pm Tue-Sat*

Petiscos & Snacks

A Venda ❸

21 C3

Mismatched decor, tiles, ceramic plates and photos decorate this cosy dining room, specialising in sharing plates, including vegetarian options. *1-3pm & 7-10pm Mon-Sat*

A Tasca do Joao ❸

22 D4

With a handful of fountain-facing tables on a square, this is a pretty spot for small-plates, cured meats, cheese and quality wines. *5-11pm Mon-Sat*

Fresh & Unfussy Seafood

O Chalavar ❸

23 A1

In this low-key, *azulejo*-decorated restaurant, select your freshly caught fish and seafood straight from the ice counter before sitting. *noon-2.30pm & 7-10pm Mon-Sat*

União dos Amigos ❸

24 A1

Local snack bar serving affordable fresh fish. *noon-3pm & 6-10pm Tue-Sun*

Memorable Meals

Los Locos ❸❸

25 C3

Imaginative, market-fresh Portuguese fusion dishes served on a mural-decorated pedestrianised street with occasional live jazz. *5-11pm Tue-Sun*

Grand Café Aliança ❸❸

26 C3

This nearly century-old cafe is Faro's grandest lunch spot. *noon-11pm Wed-Sun*

Cantinho ❸❸

27 C5

Traditional dishes, including quality *cataplanas* (including the elusive one-person option) on the pavement alongside Arco do Repouso. *noon-10pm Mon-Sat*

EPICUR ❸❸❸

28 D4

Jorge's innovative fusion dishes are paired perfectly with exceptional wines in the pocket-sized restaurant or the speakeasy-like, set-menu food club hidden behind a fridge door. *6-11pm Mon-Sat*

Vegetarian Picks

Outro Lado ❸❸

29 B3

Perfect for vegetarian versions of Portuguese favourites, such as the *francesinha* (a traditionally meat-heavy sandwich from Porto) and 'Algarvian fish stew'. *7-10pm Tue-Sat*

True Food €€

 C3

The international menu focuses on inspired and well-presented vegan and vegetarian dishes with gluten-free options. *noon-10pm Thu-Mon*

Coastal Cuisine

Café do Zé €

 B5

Beyond Praia de Faro's road-facing restaurants, this simple snack bar offers a beachfront light lunch. *9am-5pm Tue-Sun*

Estaminé €€€

see 5 C6

This architectural stunner of a restaurant at Ilha Deserta, plates sensational seafood dishes and local oysters. *noon-5pm*

Drinking

Wine & Cocktails

LAB Terrace

 B5

Arrive early to snag a front-row deckchair at this chilled-out sunset bar with uninterrupted, front-row Ria Formosa views and regular jazz trios. *4-10pm*

Varandas

 C4

Classy yet chilled three-floor cocktail bar with a snug rooftop along Vila Adentro's outer walls, mixing interesting own-recipe cocktails and drinks with great tunes. *9pm-3am*

Bago Wine Bar

 C5

Enjoy Algarvian and Portuguese wines while admiring elegant Palacete Belmarço. *11am-11pm Tue-Sat*

Craft Beers

Boheme

 B3

Sample Portugal's ever-growing craft beer scene with knowledgeable recommendations at this diminutive bar near the marina. *11am-2am*

Algarve Rock

 A1

This craft brewery's tap room serves standard and interesting-infused regional brews like piri-piri. Tours and tastings are bookable on Wednesdays. *10am-4pm Mon-Thu, to 9pm Fri*

Dancing & Live Music

Associação Recreativa e Cultural de Músicos

 C5

DJs and bands regularly perform in this open-air courtyard inside a former beer factory. *hours vary*

Palimpsestu Art Bar

 C3

Intimate, cosy and creative venue with vintage furniture and a mishmash of lamps hosting regular DJ sets and live entertainment. *6pm-1am*

Shopping

Art & Handicrafts

GAMA RAMA

 B3

Small gallery-cum-shop selling contemporary designs and hosting occasional artistic workshops. *11am-5pm Tue-Sat*

Casa da Bli

 D3

Portuguese-brand shop stocking handmade souvenirs, soaps, ceramics, textiles and homeware from various artists. *10am-8pm Mon-Sat*

Local Produce

About Wine

 D2

Buy your Portuguese wine from this independent store and enjoy personalised wine recommendations and samples. *10.30am-1pm Mon-Sat & 3-7.30pm Mon-Fri*

★ WORTH A TRIP

Estoi

Charming and tranquil Estoi, 10km northeast of Faro, remains a delightfully local-feeling Algarvian village. It's worth a half-day visit to explore the 18th-century Palácio de Estoi, see its sumptuous gardens, tour the open-air Roman ruins of Milreu, and experience the Algarve's laid-back side.

PLANNING TIPS
Vamus' daily 65 bus departing Faro at 1.45pm and returning at 6pm affords a full visit. Garden entrance fees are mandatory on Sundays. Milreu's ruins close on Mondays and over lunch.

Scan this QR code for a guide to the palace's interior.

Roman Ruins of Milreu

When archaeologists unearthed the vast **Roman ruins of Milreu** (*patrimoniocultural.gov.pt; adult/concessions €2/€1; cash*), a 15-minute walk from Estoi's centre, they were confident they had discovered a village. Following excavations, it was confirmed as the site of an extensive, luxurious villa. Inhabited by high-society families from the 1st to the 10th centuries before becoming a cemetery under Moorish rule, the site has some well-preserved details. The intact fish-depicting mosaics and former temple are particularly impressive, aided by a series of panels portraying how the crumbling walls and pools would have looked in their heyday. Some of the site's marble sculptures and artefacts are displayed in Faro's **Museu Municipal** (p40)and in Palácio de Estoi.

Palácio de Estoi & Gardens

The 18th-century **Palácio de Estoi** (*pousadas.pt; €3-5*) is a lavish former nobleman's palace. Blending baroque and rococo with neo-Moorish touches and a salmon-hued facade, the stately home is now a luxury hotel – though it's equally known for its well-manicured, decorative gardens. There are two ways to visit the grounds: free and paid. The no-charge option (except Sundays, when entrance is only via the hotel) is to access the municipal-managed gardens via the green gate on the pedestrianised road

Roman ruins of Milreu
STEPHEN POWER/SHUTTERSTOCK

left of the church. While this doesn't allow entrance to the upper gardens, you'll see the sculptures, fountain, and *azulejo*-lined staircase, where you can peek into the hotel's grounds. Alternatively, visit the palace between 11am and 6pm to tour the upper gardens and nose around inside. Three regal halls, the chapel, and a few other areas displaying historical items are visitable with the admission ticket, while guided tours (*€15*) are more in-depth. Access is complimentary with a lunch reservation.

Around the Village

Estoi's compact cluster of cobbled streets are a charming, brief wander. If open, peek inside the restored, now neoclassical-fronted **Igreja Matriz de Estoi** before buying *conserves* (canned fish), regional wines, locally produced spirits and products at **Canastra**.

TAKE A BREAK
The church-facing snack bar has the prettiest views, but nearby **La Bodeguita Del Medio** (*6.30am to 10pm*) feels more local, serving soups, toasted sandwiches and *bifanas* (pork sandwiches) all day.

Walk Olhão

Olhão long outgrew its fishing village origins, but it remains one of the Algarve's most steadfast settlements, partly due to hosting the region's largest fishing port. Before heading to the Ria Formosa's islands, spend a few hours exploring Olhão's Cubist architecture, statues and murals, and typical neighbourhoods.

START	END	LENGTH
Rua da Fábrica Velha	O Sardines Restaurant	4.4km; 1½ hours

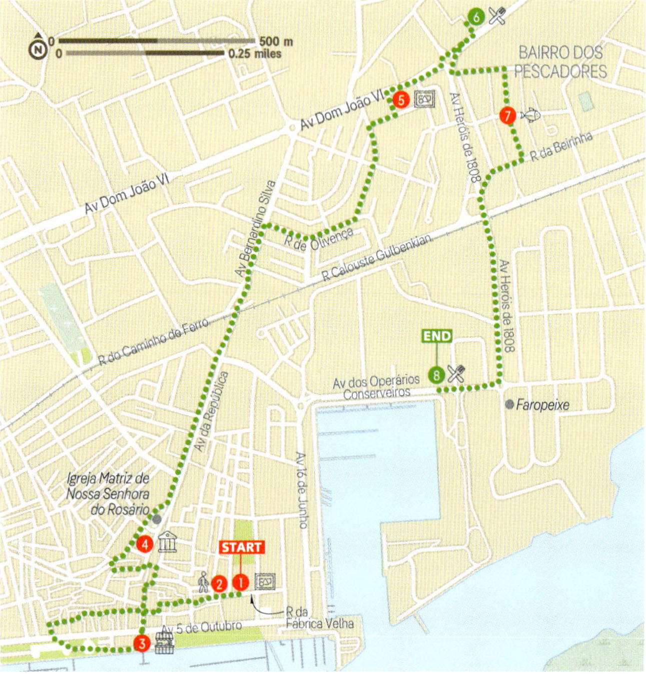

1 Magnificent Murals

Start at the dilapidated factories along Rua da Fábrica Velha coated with **spectacular monochrome murals** depicting scenes of yore, including canning factory workers and fishermen's get-togethers.

2 Trail of Legends

Track the **Caminho das Lendas** (Legends Path), weaving through narrow cobbled streets bound by Olhão's signature low-rise Cubist homes, tracing five storytelling statues depicting a different legendary local character.

3 Market Mornings

Turning to the waterfront, visit the century-old **Mercados de Olhão** (7am to 2pm Monday to Saturday), a pair of red-brick buildings hawking fresh fish and farmers produce. In front is a replica of the **Caíque Bom Sucesso**, which sailed to Brazil following the 1808 expulsion of French troops.

4 Historic Sights

Follow the pedestrianised streets with colourful boat bow plant pots towards **Praça da Restauração**'s pair of churches and a small museum. If open, climb **Igreja Matriz de Nossa Senhora do Rosário**'s tower to appreciate Olhão's Cubist layout. The rear blue-and-white azulejo chapel is visible anytime.

5 Street Art

Continue on **Avenida da República**, lined with grand buildings from the town's 20th-century fishing boom. Pause at the fountain-fronted rural azulejo scene and the mosaic-adorned courthouse. Turn right onto Rua de Olivença for more colourful murals, particularly **Vivenda Vitória**, an abandoned stately home plastered in graffiti.

6 Sweet Treat

Folar de Olhão, a bread-like cake layered with cinnamon and sugar, is a cherished local treat. Near the supermarket, a ramp leads to **João Mendes & Rita** (9am to 6pm Monday to Friday), a factory famed for its production. Knock to buy (cash only) a freshly baked cake.

7 Fishermen's Neighbourhood

Cross the road to enter the residential **Bairro dos Pescadores** (Fishermen's Neighbourhood), with typical single-storey terraced homes and staircases leading to net-drying rooftops. From here, follow the flyover (there's a small side path) towards the waterfront.

8 Sardine Stops

At the roundabout with a canning worker statue, cross to **Faropeixe** (9am to 6pm Monday to Friday) to shop for *conserves* (canned fish) or turn right to roadside O Sardines (noon to 9pm Monday to Friday) for unfussy seasonal sardines or grilled fish before heading to the islands.

★ WORTH A TRIP

The Ria Formosa

Encompassing flamingo-frequented salt pans, birdlife-harbouring marshy wetlands and idyllic barrier islands, the **Parque Natural da Ria Formosa** is phenomenal. Extending 60km between **Quinta do Lago** and **Cacela Velha**, it can be daunting knowing where to start. Thankfully, much can be experienced without a formal boat tour.

PLANNING TIPS
Olhão is the Ria Formosa's de facto main gateway. The Olhão Train Station is 1km from the waterfront; a large, paid car park (*€3.50/day*) is just east of the ferry pier.

Scan this QR code to learn more about the Ria Formosa's ecosystems.

Birdwatching & Wildlife

Flamingos, curlews, seahorses, Mediterranean chameleons, spoonbills, the purple swamphen – the park's symbol – and more call the Ria Formosa home, especially in the winter and migration seasons. An excellent starting point to learn about the park and its wildlife is **Quinta de Marim** (*icnf.pt; €3; closed weekends*), a Roman-founded estate that hosts the **Centro de Educação Ambiental de Marim**. Extensive English information panels inside pair with a 2.5km trail through the protected area, which meets mixed ecosystems and birdlife. The **Passadicos de Loule** (p41) boardwalk near Faro is another easy birdwatching amble. On the water, a kayak is a good DIY way to see lagoon birdlife, while guided boat trips afford more expert insights. **Lands**' (*lands.pt; from €40*) quieter, less disturbing solar boats depart from Faro. Dolphins are occasionally seen in the lagoon, but **cetacean tours** (p41) beyond the barrier islands provide a better chance of sightings.

Island-Hopping by Boat

Five car-free, silky sanded and dune-laced barrier islands separate the lagoon's slightly warmer waters from the Atlantic. From west to east, they are **Ilha da**

Purple swamphen

TONY MILLS/SHUTTERSTOCK ©

Barreta (often called **Ilha Deserta**), **Ilha da Culatra** (including **Ilha do Farol**, frequently presented as distinct islands), **Ilha da Armona**, **Ilha de Tavira** and **Ilha de Cabanas**. All are reachable by ferry; the departure points to the main island beaches are **Faro** (p35), **Tavira** (p55) and **Olhão** (p48).

The two inhabited central islands, **Ilha da Culatra** and **Ilha da Armona**, have restaurants, facilities and undersized bungalow-style settlements and are best accessed via Olhão's **Cais de Embarque** (*adult/child from €2/€1 one-way, cash-only*). Ferries depart every two to three hours during daylight. To buy tickets for the 20- to 30-minute trip, queue at the correct hut (there are two separate, adjacent ticket desks), which usually opens around 30 minutes before departure. It can be crowded over summer weekends, and the last ferry is always packed. Sometimes, additional return ferries are added but not guaranteed, so

OVERNIGHT STAYS

Some islands have accommodation, including Armona's Orbitur bungalows, Tavira's campsite and Barco Casa's handful of solar-powered houseboats anchored off the islands.

LUNCH STOP
On Armona, enjoy a dune-view cocktail or fresh fish lunch at **Lanacosta** (*Tuesday to Sunday*) or book **chá chá chá** (*Tuesday to Saturday*) in Olhão for unfiltered wines, reimagined traditional dishes and vegetarian options.

it's best to arrive early as water taxis are costly. Island-hopping between Armona and Culatra requires a return to Olhão. Some ferries have ramps (best confirmed when purchasing tickets), and Faro-based **Ria Formosa Boat Tours** (*riaformosaboatours.com; prices vary*) operates a customised, wheelchair-accessible vessel with a water hoist. **MárioSUP**'s (*mariosup.wixsite.com/mariosup; prices vary*) kayak and SUP tours from Olhão, Fuseta or Tavira offer a more active way to reach the islands.

Ferry-Free Beaches

If you'd prefer boat-free beaches, **Praia de Faro** (p40) has road access, **Praia do Barril** (p63), with its anchor cemetery, can be reached by foot or a teeny **tourist train** via a bridge, and at low tide, many people paddle to pretty **Praia da Cacela Velha** (p65), although fishing boats also depart from nearby. One of the finest lagoon-side beaches is **Praia da Fuseta Ria** (train station Fuseta-A), particularly at low tide when swirling sands and shallow cyan waters allow foot access to its iconic lifeguard station.

Fishing & Festivals

Licensing controls fishing in the Ria Formosa for bass and bream, harvesting clams and cockles by hand, and oyster farming. Some of the best people-watching occurs at low tide when licensed fishers hand dig for clams, and Culatra's oyster farms can be better appreciated. To see buckets of freshly caught clams, smaller conquilhas and oysters – many of which are farmed for the French market – and the fishers in action, wander around the fishing huts beside Culatra village on the island's north. **Artur's Watersports** (*arturwatersportsacademy.pt; prices vary*) offers a Faro-departing day trip on a traditional fishing boat, which includes harvesting clams and sampling Culatra's oysters. In mid-August, Olhão – home to the Algarve's largest fishing port and main seafood market **Mercados de Olhão** (p49) – hosts the five-day **Festival do Marisco** (*festivaldomarisco.com*), animated with seafood stalls, traditional recipes and live music.

Salt Pans

Working *salinas* (salt pans) speckle the mainland facing the Ria Formosa, providing economic benefits and birdlife havens, especially for now-resident flamingos. Certain combinations of minerals and algae occasionally turn the tapestry of rectangles vivid colours, including pink. Hire a bike or join a tour at **SeaHorse Bike Rental** (*seahorsebikerental.com; from €14*) to explore Olhão's *salinas* or book direct at **Salinas do Grelha** (*salinasdogrelha.pt; from €8*) for salt-production tours and to float in the **Mar Morto** (Dead Sea) between May and October.

VISITING RESPONSIBLY

A Code of Conduct protects the ecosystems of the natural park. To help preserve the environment, avoid walking on sand dunes or partaking in unlicensed clam harvesting, don't touch chameleons, and opt for non-motorised activities, such as kayaking, whenever possible. In recent years, the resident seahorse population has decreased by 90%; avoid tours that swim or interact with the species.

See p66
for eating,
drinking and
shopping
listings

Explore
Tavira & Around

Since the Phoenicians introduced their tuna-catching almadrava nets millennia ago, Tavira has been steadily packed with maritime methods, monuments, and the legacy of all who have been and gone. Pinnacling as the Algarve's most populated town, thanks to a flourishing 16th-century North African trade, Tavira's eminence was eroded by earthquakes, a plague and the dying bluefin tuna fishing industry – now memorialised in bite-size museums and a beachfront anchor graveyard. With whitewashed cobbled streets, garden squares, concert-hosting churches, idyllic islands and a laid-back Mediterranean lifestyle, it remains one of the Algarve's most authentic destinations, with the Eastern Algarve's sweeping sands just beyond.

Getting Around

Bus

Tavira's centre is very walkable and supported by two local bus routes. Vamus buses depart from the riverside terminal to Santa Luzia, Luz, Cabanas and beyond. Use ferries for the islands.

Cycling

Marked road lanes to Santa Luzia and the car-free Ciclovia to Cabanas make cycling delightful.

Train

Tavira and Porta Nova stations are under 1km from Tavira's centre. Though Luz, Cacela and Monte Gordo have stations, buses pass closer.

Tavira
ISRAEL RUIZ/SHUTTERSTOCK ©

THE BEST

CULTURAL EXPERIENCE Fado com História (p58)

BIRDLIFE Salt pan flamingo sightings (p63)

BEACH Ilha de Tavira (p63)

ACTIVITY Taste Algarve's cooking class (p62)

PANORAMA Cacela Velha (p65)

A
B
C
D
1
2
3
4
5
6
0 4 km
0 2 miles
For more see
Top Experiences p58
Experiences p62
Eating p66
Drinking p67
Shopping p67
Parque de Lazer do Perímetro Florestal da Conceição de Tavira
Ribeira da Zambujosa
Ribeira da Gafa
Ribeira do Almargem
Via do Infante
Cacela Velha
Parque Natural da Ria Formosa
27
24
Tavira Equestrian Tourism
FÁBRICA
25
Praia de Cacela Velha
CONCEIÇÃO
Praia do Lacém
35
CABANAS DE TAVIRA
17
Ilha de Cabanas
23 Atelier Medronho
See Tavira Enlargement
Hélder Madeira Olive Oil Cooperative
20
9 Ciclovia de Tavira
7 Taste Algarve
32
TAVIRA
Tavira
49
Arraial Ferreira
6 Neto Museum
Quatro Águas 8
13
Quarto Aguas Ferry Terminal 40
11
Praia da Ilha de Tavira
21
36
Parque Natural da Ria Formosa
Santa Luzia 22
Praia da Terra Estreita
19 Mini Train
18 Praia do Barril
ATLANTIC OCEAN

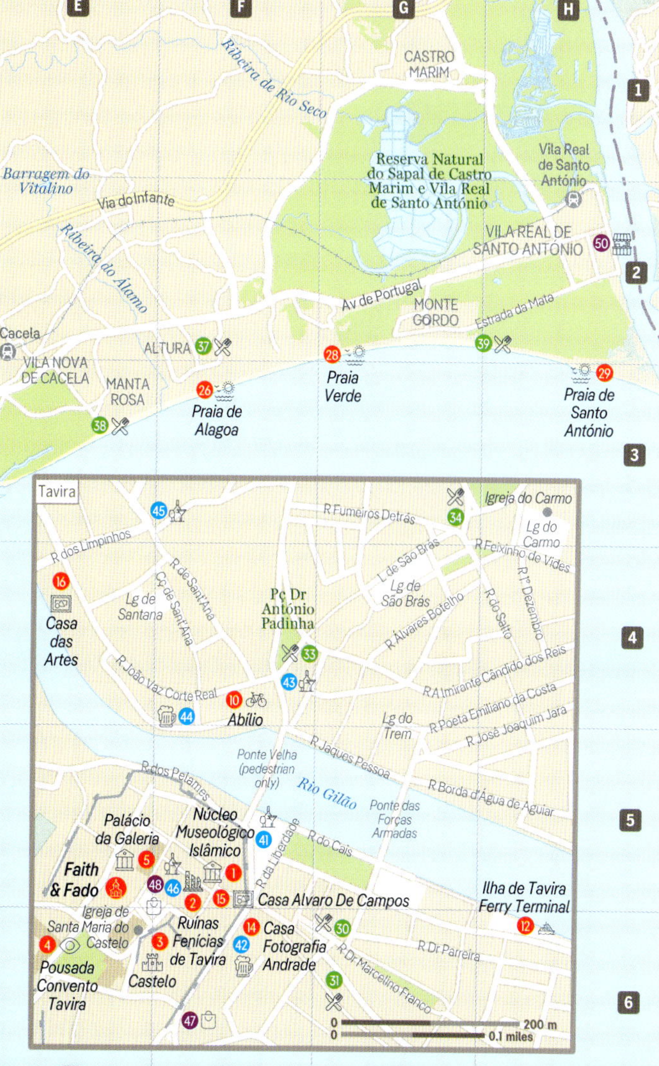
E
F
G
H
1
2
3
4
5
6
Ribeira de Rio Seco
CASTRO MARIM
Reserva Natural do Sapal de Castro Marim e Vila Real de Santo António
Vila Real de Santo António
VILA REAL DE SANTO ANTÓNIO
50
Barragem do Vitalino
Via do Infante
Ribeira do Álamo
Av de Portugal
MONTE GORDO
Estrada da Mata
Cacela
VILA NOVA DE CACELA
ALTURA
37
MANTA ROSA
38
26
Praia de Alagoa
28
Praia Verde
39
29
Praia de Santo António
Tavira
45
R Fumeiros Detrás
34
Igreja do Carmo
Lg do Carmo
R Feixinho de Vides
R dos Limpinhos
16
Casa das Artes
R de Sant'Ana
Cç de Sant'Ana
Lg de Santana
Pç Dr António Padinha
L de São Brás
Lg de São Brás
R Álvares Botelho
R do Salto
R 1º Dezembro
33
43
R João Vaz Corte Real
10
Abílio
44
R Almirante Cândido dos Reis
R Poeta Emiliano da Costa
R José Joaquim Jara
Lg do Trem
R Jaques Pessoa
Ponte Velha (pedestrian only)
Rio Gilão
R dos Pelames
Ponte das Forças Armadas
R Borda d'Água de Aguiar
Palácio da Galeria
5
Núcleo Museológico Islâmico
41
R da Liberdade
R do Cais
1
Faith & Fado
48
46
2
15
Casa Alvaro De Campos
Ilha de Tavira Ferry Terminal
12
Igreja de Santa Maria do Castelo
4
Pousada Convento Tavira
3
Ruínas Fenícias de Tavira
Castelo
14
Casa Fotografia Andrade
42
30
R Dr Parreira
R Dr Marcelino Franco
31
47
0
200 m
0
0.1 miles

★ TOP EXPERIENCE

Faith & Fado

Tavira's moniker as the 'City of Churches' is well deserved. Over 30 religious buildings in all sizes and styles are found around the Old Town. Some serve as museums, while many host performances of fado, Portugal's melancholic and expressive musical genre. These are the standouts.

PLANNING TIP
Smaller churches have sporadic opening hours, though all pause visits for Sunday Mass. The main churches offer fixed, combined entrance tickets costing €3 (one), €7 (three) and €10 (five).

Scan this QR code for a guide to all of Tavira's churches.

Fado Concerts

Fado com História (*fadocomhistoria.com; €10*) holds one-hour afternoon performances, including a fado history video introduction, Mondays to Saturdays. Concerts are in the magnificent Igreja da Misericórdia or the next-door auditorium. Book online to check which venue is being used. Some smaller churches, such as **Ermida de São Sebastião**, with its intricately hand-painted wooden panels, host more intimate concerts on Saturdays. During July and August, **Jardim do Coreto**'s bandstand usually hosts weekly al fresco, late-evening performances.

Church Museums

Only have time to visit one? Make it 16th-century **Igreja da Misericórdia**. Open daily, the back rooms serve as a museum, the bell tower provides city views and the azulejo-adorned main hall is swoon-worthy. **Igreja de Santa Maria do Castelo**, constructed on the site of the old mosque, also has intricate tile work and a sacred treasury, while 15th-century **Igreja De São José**, a former religious hospital, has history-telling multimedia displays in its side rooms.

Igreja da Misericórdia
LUX BLUE/SHUTTERSTOCK ©

Worth A Visit

Igreja do Carmo is one of the city's most impressive, with exquisite carvings and highly artistic baroque and rococo decor. Sadly, it's usually closed unless you're attending Mass. Nearby, the **Chapel of Nossa Senhora do Livramento** is similar, though its main draw is the blue-and-white azulejo facade. Near the castle, **Igreja de Santiago**'s original structure dates from the 13th-century Moorish period, though much that appears today – including the splashy golden medallion on its facade – is from the 18th-century reconstruction.

EAT & SLEEP
For a more intimate experience, stay overnight or enjoy a meal at the 16th-century **Pousada Convento Tavira**. The spectacular, cloister-anchored space was once a convent for Augustinian Nuns.

WALKING TOUR

Walk Tavira

One of Portugal's first Phoenician settlements with preceding Bronze Age history, Tavira is one of the Algarve's oldest – and prettiest – towns. Touring its cluster of historical sights is brief, but make time to detour down whitewashed streets illuminated by bougainvillaea and paint-rimmed traditional wooden doors.

START	END	LENGTH
Mercado Municipal	Jardim da Alagoa	2.8km; 1¼ hours

1 Market Mornings

As one of the region's larger, more local-feeling markets, **Mercado Municipal** is an excellent introduction to why Tavira is Portugal's UNESCO representative of the Mediterranean diet. Cafes serve breakfast.

2 Books & Bibles

Walk alongside Convento das Bernardas, a former Manueline-style convent turned factory and now residences, towards **Biblioteca Álvaro de Campos** (Tuesday to Friday). A former jail, it's now an architecturally attractive library with a cafe inside. Opposite, find one of Tavira's more intimate churches, **Ermida de São Sebastião**.

3 Riverside Garden

After weaving through charming residential backstreets, you'll reach the riverside. Stroll through the recovered 19th-century **Mercado da Ribeira** and leafy **Jardim do Coreto** with its moat-hemmed bandstand, perhaps pausing for an ice cream from Fábrica Do Meu Avô. Adjacent is **Praca da Republica**, Tavira's main square with cafes and a small amphitheatre.

4 Islamic Relics

The small collection of Islamic artefacts at the Núcleo Museológico Islâmico doesn't take long to visit. Next door, the **Porta de D. Manuel** stone archway, part of the former city walls, leads to the Old Town. Enter here, or continue along shop-lined Rua da Liberdade to the **Escadinhas do Castelo** (Castle's Stairs).

5 Ruins & Views

Climb the stairs to the Moorish crenellated **Castelo**, with its panoramic views and Phoenician ruins below. In the 16th-century Pousada Convento, some of the 12th-century Moorish neighbourhood's foundations are visible.

6 Grand Buildings

Descending towards the river, you'll pass a trio of impressive buildings: the **Igreja de Santa Maria do Castelo**, museum-like, fado-hosting **Igreja da Misericórdia**, and the **Palácio da Galeria**, now the Museu Municipal.

7 Across The Gilão

Cross the river on the seven-arched, 17th-century **Ponte Velha**. The original is believed to have been constructed by the Romans as an integral trade route to **Balsa** (p63).

8 Leafy Lunch

Across the river, artisan shops and riverside bars await. Enjoy lunch around **Jardim da Alagoa**, with views of Igreja do Convento de São Paulo.

EXPERIENCES

Admire Islamic Artefacts

MUSEUM

MAP: 1 P56 F5

Constructed around a 12th-century, rammed-earth Moorish wall, the **Núcleo Museológico Islâmico** (*cm-tavira.pt; €2*), closed on Sundays and Mondays, displays locally discovered Islamic artefacts. It takes 30 minutes to see the whole collection, including the 11th-century Tavira Vase, a red clay vessel adorned with mini figurines depicting a ceremonial bridal abduction. Exhibits are in Portuguese; request a translated booklet from reception. There's step-free access and a lift to the second floor.

Explore Tavira's Layered History

ARCHAEOLOGICAL SITES

Museums aside, Tavira's history is told through archaeological sites, with three practically side by side. The **Ruínas Fenícias de Tavira** (MAP: 2 P56 F5) confirm the Phoenicians' presence; a 13m stretch of their 8th-century-BCE wall is visible through a fence. Nearby, the Moorish crenellated **Castelo** (MAP: 3 P56 F6), reconstructed in the 17th century, now shelters a botanical garden while the walls and tower afford far-reaching views. Behind is where the Almohad Quarter would have been, and inside the **Pousada Convento Tavira** (MAP: 4 P56 E6), now a hotel, a small museum preserves an excavated part of the 12th-century neighbourhood.

Delve into the Mediterranean & Local Diet

MUSEUMS/FESTIVALS

As Portugal's representative to UNESCO's cross-nation Intangible Cultural Heritage of the Mediterranean Diet, Tavira abounds with age-old culinary practices. The **Palácio da Galeria** (MAP: 5 P56 E5; *cm-tavira.pt; €2*), closed on Sundays and Mondays, hosts an exhibition dedicated to the Mediterranean Diet's UNESCO listing, explaining why this Atlantic country is culturally Mediterranean. A second museum, the teeny **Arraial Ferreira Neto** (MAP: 6 P56 B4; inside the Hotel Vila Galé Albacora), focuses on Tavira's tuna history, displaying models of boats and the Phoenicians' complex almadrava nets, used up until the tuna fishing industry collapsed in the 20th century. In early September, the **Mediterranean Diet Fair** celebrates local culture and cuisine, as does May's **Festival de Gastronomia do Mar**, when restaurants serve local catch and traditional dishes.

Learn Local Recipes in a Quinta

COOKING CLASS

MAP: 7 P56 A4

For a hands-on dive into local flavours, learn regional recipes at **Taste Algarve**'s (*tastealgarve.com; from €110*) cooking classes hosted at a fourth-generation family farm outside the city. Led by ever-knowledgeable Inês, the pre-bookable group experiences include a farm tour, with vines, carob and fig trees; morning classes feature a market visit. There's a brief hello to Malha, their adorable donkey, before entering the modern kitchen and learning how to prepare a traditional three-course meal. The always-requested *cataplana* is usually on the menu. Hard work done, settle into the panoramic terrace overlooking Tavira and the ocean to savour your labour. Class-free lunches and dinners are also available.

Spot Flamingos in the Salinas

SALT PANS

Tavira's *salinas* (salt pans) flank both sides of the Rio Gilão, with records dating salt production to the 4th century BCE. Small ridges on the **Quatro Águas** (MAP: 8 P56 B5) side allow for closer inspection near Rui Simeon's production area. Across the river, the **Ciclovia de Tavira** (MAP: 9 P56, B4) leading to Cabanas, is bike suitable (**Abílio** is a reliable rental spot; MAP: 10 P56 F4). Juvenile flamingos, terns and spoonbills can be seen depending on the season. Vivid pink pools appear when the algae concentration aligns.

Take the Ferry to Ilha de Tavira

ISLAND

Trade sightseeing for sunbathing by hopping on the 20-minute ferry to **Praia da Ilha de Tavira** (MAP: 11 P56 B5), an idyllic, dune-laced island beach backed by pine forests. Ferries depart roughly every hour in daylight from the spring-to-autumn riverside **Ilha de Tavira Ferry Terminal** (MAP: 12 P56 H6; *silnido.com; adult/child €2.50/€1.10 return*) with salt pan views, while the **Quarto Aguas Ferry Terminal** (MAP: 13 P56 B5) is year-round. On the beach, find a handful of restaurants and a seasonal concession offering massages and parasols.

Seek Nearby Shorelines

BEACHES

Similarly priced seasonal ferries connect **Ilha de Cabanas** (MAP: 17 P56 C4; which can have long summer queues due to small boats) and **Santa Luzia** to their respective island beaches. **Praia do Barril** (see 18 P56 A6) and its curious collection of ageing anchors assembled to honour the extinct tuna fishing industry is accessed via a 1.5km

THE ROMAN CITY OF BALSA

Discovered by archaeologist Estácio da Veiga in 1866, most of the roughly 46-hectare Roman city of Balsa remains buried in present-day Luz de Tavira. The only easily visible part is Torre de Aires, a Moorish stone watchtower believed to be built atop a Roman base. Periodic ongoing excavations have unearthed glassware, coins, tanks for producing garum (fish sauce), necropolises and mosaics. Sadly, many artefacts remain in storage. Following Tavira's excellent but temporary 2024 Balsa exhibition in the Palácio da Galeria, it is hoped the growing collection will earn a permanent home.

BEST ART GALLERIES

Casa Fotografia Andrade

MAP: 14 P56 F6

In this small museum above a photo studio, fourth-generation Miguel Andrade shares his great-grandfather's vintage equipment and images capturing the Algarve of old (€5).

Casa Alvaro De Campos

MAP: 15 P56 F5

Compact gallery and cultural venue hosting musical recitals and occasional English-language talks.

Casa das Artes

MAP: 16 P56 E4

Appreciate after-dark art at this evening-only gallery, hosting temporary exhibitions in a sociable environment.

trail or aboard the **Mini Train** (MAP: 19 P56 A6; €2). To the island's west is aptly named **Praia do Homem Nu** (Naked Man Beach), an official nudist beach. Pricier water taxis are available to most island beaches.

Tour an Olive Grove

FACTORY

MAP: 20 P56 B4

There's no need to leave Tavira to taste local liquid gold. **Hélder Madeira Olive Oil Cooperative** (*heldermadeira.com; €17.50*) runs 90-minute tours and tastings with typical local produce at 4pm daily (excluding Thursdays and Sundays) in their central factory. For the full grove experience, drive 20 minutes to **Monterosa Olive Oil** (MAP: 21 P56 A5 *monterosa-olive oil.com; adult/child €14/€7.50*), one of the Algarve's premier producers of extra virgin olive oils. Their prebookable 75-minute morning tours and tastings run Tuesday to Friday and include a stroll through the olive trees before visiting the pressing factory to taste three distinct olive oils.

Sample Octopus in Santa Luzia

SEAFOOD

MAP: 22 P56 A5

The estuary-facing village of **Santa Luzia** is now practically a suburb of Tavira. Known as Portugal's unofficial octopus capital, the waters fronting the town are a prime place for capturing *polvo* (octopus) using centuries-old *alcatruzes* (octopus-catching clay pots). However, they have mainly been phased out in favour of modern alternatives. Head to the fishermen's huts east of the village in the morning to see the catch; the not-public auction market usually happens before 11am. Information boards trace the Octopus Route, while restaurants such as **Casa do Polvo** (p66) prepare and cook the speciality countless ways.

Taste the Local Firewater

DISTILLERY

MAP: 23 P56 **B4**

In a residential part of town, André offers pre-scheduled visits to his intimate, small-batch *aguardente*-brewing **Atelier Medronho** (*ateliermedronho@gmail.com*) studio. Over 45 minutes, he'll explain the fermentation process of the *medronho* tree's red berries while serving you suitably strong samples of the Algarve's infamous firewater.

Visit the Algarve's Prettiest Hamlet

VILLAGE

MAP: 24 P56 **D3**

It's subjective, but the panorama from clifftop **Cacela Velha** is arguably the Algarve's most sublime coastal view, especially at low tide when swirling sands are laced with all shades of blue. Take it in from the whitewashed walls fronting the teeny, time-capsule-like village – the 17th-century fort (closed to the public) adds to the photogenic appeal. A staircase beside the cemetery descends to the water, and while not officially advised, many people paddle to **Praia de Cacela Velha**'s sandbar (MAP: 25 P56 D3) at low tide; strandings happen when the water level rises. Alternatively, boats depart from nearby Fábrica. In the village, it only takes ten minutes to admire the old well, whitewashed church, and residential homes hemmed in azure blue, before devouring fresh seafood at **Casa da Igreja** (p67).

Explore the Eastern Algarve's Coast

BEACH TOWNS

To the east of Tavira, a handful of towns back the uninterrupted sands stretching from Manta Rota to the **Guadiana River** (p68). Altura's **Praia de Alagoa** (MAP: 26 P56 F3) is one of the most accessible, with flat boardwalks, shore-accessing walkways and seasonal amphibious wheelchairs available. **Tavira Equestrian Tourism** (MAP: 27 P56 D3; *taviraequestriantourism.com; prices vary*) offers guided horse rides at low tide along these eastern beaches, and the pine forest trails leading to **Praia Verde** (MAP: 28 P56 G2) and **Praia de Santo António** (MAP: 29 P56 H3), the Algarve's easternmost beach, make for pleasant shaded strolls. **Monte Gordo**, with ample nightlife and a casino, is the liveliest.

ALTA MORA'S ALMOND BLOSSOMS

Alta Mora, 30 minutes from Tavira, is a rural hamlet hideaway. Yet, all changes for a few weeks over January and February when the surrounding almond trees blossom, and the 11.5km **Caminho da Amendoeira** (PR8) becomes one of the region's most sought-after trails. During the period, the villagers host a fantastic three-day celebration, the **Algarve Almond Blossom Festival** (*facebook.com/festivalamendoeiras; €3*), with guided walks, performances, traditional craft exhibits and the baking of a humongous almond pie.

LISTINGS

Best Places for...

See p56 for map of locations

€ Budget €€ Midrange €€€ Top End

Eating

Cafes & Sweet Treats

Lá Calha €
 see 49
Join traders and fishers outside the market at this simple snack bar for early beers and *bifanas* (pork steak sandwiches). *7am-5pm Mon-Sat*

Pastelaria Tavirense €
 30 G6
Long-standing local favourite for sugary treats, including *pastéis de nata* (custard tarts) and local recipes baked with almond and carob. *7am-10pm*

Traditional Dishes

Romba €
31 G6
Mediterranean meat and fish dishes (including delicious juicy garlic prawns) presented with personality; grab a countertop seat for some local tips. *noon-3pm & 6-9pm, Mon-Sat*

Jorge e Lia €€
 32 A4
This tranquil, couple-run restaurant is worth a walk from the centre for top-notch tuna steaks and wholesome hospitality in the hidden rear garden. *noon-10pm Mon-Sat*

Ponto de Encontro €€
 33 F4
Reliable choice for octopus, tender steaks and whole grilled fish on one of Tavira's prettiest squares. *noon-2.30pm & 7-9.30pm Wed-Mon*

Ti Maria €€
 34 G3
Sample a selection of interesting, regional sharing plates at this cute tapas bar with a spacious terrace. *noon-1am Mon-Sat*

Reservation Worthy Restaurants

Noélia €€
 35 C4
Celebrity chef Noélia Jerónimo crafts first-class and fair-priced Algarvian seafood dishes (the oyster rice is sublime) in her self-named Cabanas de Tavira restaurant. *12.30pm-3pm & 7-10pm Thu-Tue*

A Carpintaria €€
 36 A5
Enjoy elevated Algarvian cuisine on a terrace soundtracked by birds or in the homely fireplace dining room of this Luz de Tavira eatery. The *porco à Alentejana* (pork and clams) is flawless. *11am-10pm Tue-Sat*

Casa do Polvo €€
 see 22
Octopus countless ways in an institution of a restaurant overlooking the fishing waters of Santa Luzia. *noon-2.45pm & 6.30-9.30pm, Wed-Mon*

East Coast Seafood

Dois Irmãos €
37 F2
A short walk from Altura's beach, this popular and often packed local favourite is the go-to lunch spot for grilled fish. *9am-5pm Mon-Sat*

Chá Com Água Salgada €€
 38 E3
In Manta Rota, Sandra and Paulo's romantic dune-facing restaurant excels at local seafood specialities, including *muxama* (cured tuna) soup and delicate, aioli-topped cod. *noon-10pm*

Casa da Igreja €€

see 

Arrive pre-opening to ensure an outside table for oysters, clams and freshly delivered seafood delights in Cacela Velha. *4.30-9.30pm Mon-Sat*

The Prime Beach Club €€

 H2

At the quieter end of Monte Gordo's beach, this seasonal restaurant has ocean views, good vibes, and varied dishes, serving brunch to seafood feasts. *10am-10pm*

Drinking

Cocktails & Views

O Ferreira

 B5

This seasonal Ilha de Tavira restaurant is also fantastic for beachside cocktails and coolers on the dune-facing bucket chairs and rattan swings. *9am-7pm*

Arcada

 F5

Dimly lit and classy bar serving competently crafted cocktails and sangria; the terrace has pleasant views of Praça da República. *11am-midnight Tue-Sun, to 2am Fri & Sat.*

Live Music

Clube De Tavira

 F6

An ornate staircase leads to an old-school hall, board games, and a funky garden terrace. Check Facebook for jazz and jam schedules. *hours vary*

Tavila Café

 F4

Often overspilling with singing patrons after dark, this small bar is a spirited spot for live bands and generously poured wines. *10am-midnight*

The Black Anchor

 F4

The vast riverside terrace of this typical Irish pub is great for a sunset pint when local singers and guitarists are often busking. *noon-1am*

Rooftop Bars

Rooftop Nomad Bar

45 F3

Sunset cocktails and sweeping views over Tavira, the salinas, and the Ria Formosa from this lofty hotel bar. *5pm-midnight*

A Ver Tavira

 F5

This Michelin-starred restaurant is an indulgence, but opt for the panoramic rooftop bar instead for a more affordable snack and cocktail menu. *noon-3pm & 7-10pm, Tue-Sat*

Shopping

Handicrafts & Ceramics

Atelier Carmo Saúde

47 F6

Step into Carmo's artisanal small gallery to browse her distinct handcrafted *azulejos* (tiles) and ceramic souvenirs. *11am-5pm Mon-Fri*

Casa do Artesão

 F5

The typical ceramics, weaving, embroidery and produce at this association-run shop near the castle are labelled with the local artist's name. *10am-5pm Mon-Fri*

Markets

Mercado Municipal

 B4

Tavira's animated main market (not to be confused with the old riverside building) is an excellent spot for fresh produce and fish alongside locally produced oils and honey. *7am-1pm Mon-Sat*

Feira de Velharias

 H2

On the second Saturday of each month, Vila Real de Santo António hosts an antiques and flea market on Praça Marquês de Pombal. *8am-5pm*

★ WORTH A TRIP

Along the Rio Guadiana

Life along the Rio Guadiana, the Algarve's natural border with Spain's Andalusia, is blissfully unhurried. Long gone are the days of Spanish aggression and smuggling, though stories and fortresses from more fraught times survive. Nowadays, river sailings, stuck-in-time settlements, serene salt pans and some surprises await.

PLANNING TIPS
Hire a car or bike, take a full-day boat trip, or hike the 66km Grande Rota do Guadiana. Vamus buses link towns but on restrictive weekday-only commuter schedules. Trains reach Vila Real de Santo António.

Scan this QR code for maps of the Rio Guadiana's walking and cycling trails.

Vila Real de Santo António

Essentially swallowed by the sea, **Vila Real de Santo António** (VRSA) was reconstructed in the 18th century using elements of Lisbon's post-earthquake grid. The city's Pombaline layout is most obvious around with its *calçadas portuguesas* (Portuguese cobblestone pavements). Spend an hour strolling around, enjoy the bi-monthly flea market, **Feira de Velharias** (p67), and visit the small **Arquivo Histórico Municipal António Rosa Mendes** (*cm-vrsa.pt*), closed Sundays, documenting VRSA's tuna canning history through packaging printing presses, model ships and traditional tools.

Upstream River Adventure

VRSA is an excellent jumping-off point to experience the navigable stretch of the Rio Guadiana. At **818 Centro Náutico** (*818.pt; prices vary*), skipper Max and his Portuguese water dog Nó (currently learning to listen for dolphins) offer private boat tours, kayak rentals and jet skis. Upstream full-day boat tours to Alcoutim are bookable with **Transguadiana** (*transguadiana.com; adult/child €63/€43*), while **Riosultravel** (*riosultravel.com; adult/child €58/€32*) organise shorter sailings to a Foz de Odeleite farmhouse lunch. In Alcoutim, **Fun**

SOPOTNICKI/SHUTTERSTOCK ©

River (*fun-river.com; €1.50 one-way*) runs a ferry to Spain's Sanlúcar de Guadiana roughly every hour from 8am to 8pm, and offers kayak rental.

Medieval Castro Marim

Casto Marim's 13th-century **Castelo** (*cm-castro marim.pt; adult/child €1.10/€0.55*) is the town's hill-topping medieval defence. Inside the walls, you can visit the original, four-towered castle, housing a miniature but alarming medieval torture museum. It's rustic and slightly overgrown; in summer, watch out for snakes. Standing on the hill opposite is the 17th-century **Forte de São Sebastião**, only visitable during **Casto Marim's Medieval Days**. The festival, hosted in the last weeks of August, sees the garrison town turn back time with mead-pouring stands, flame-wielding dancers, and period-costumed performances. Year-round, experience medieval song, dance and candlelit costumes at **Velho Cavalinho Taberna Medieval** restaurant (*11am to 7.30pm Monday to Friday, to 9.30pm Saturday*).

INLAND BATHING BREAK

Cool off inland at Alcoutim's river beach, Praia Fluvial do Pego Fundo, where the seasonal beach bar, Tá-se Bem (*10am to 10pm*), serves snacks and ice creams, and hosts bands in summer.

Salt Harvesting & Mud Spas

Fronting Castro Marim, the **Reserva Natural do Sapal de Castro Marim e Vila Real de Santo António** (around a 3km walk from VRSA train station) is a Spain-facing tapestry of salt pans and mainland Portugal's oldest nature reserve. Join Jorge at **Salmarim** (*salmarim.com; prebookings; prices vary*) to learn how to harvest premium Fleur de Sel by hand, gathering the floating crystals with an ancestral wooden net. Then, after a hard morning's work, cross the road to seasonal **Agua Maé** (*aguamae.pt; from €8*), closed Mondays and Tuesdays, for a salty mud spa experience.

The Blue Dragon River

Nicknamed for its aerial appearance, **Barragem de Odeleite** is less dramatic than its moniker implies. A calm body of water, devoid of development other than Odeleite's small hamlet, it's a

peaceful place for rambles and SUP sessions, which can be arranged, including transfers from Tavira, with **Eolis** (*kitesurfeolis.com; €80*). If the dragon-like river piques your interest, get an aerial view with **SkyXpedition**'s (*skyxpedition.com; from €99*) brief and scenic gyrocopter flights.

On The Smuggling Trail

For centuries, trade between Spain and Portugal flowed relatively freely until the 1936 Spanish Civil War. Suddenly, smuggling was rife. A booming contraband business saw tobacco, coffee, cognac and perfumes hauled across the river in sacks during the dead of night. Many contrabandistas were caught, bribes were paid, and the sister towns of **Alcoutim** and Sanlúcar de Guadiana – where the river is narrowest – developed a unique relationship. Every other year, in March or April, this shared history is relived over the three-day **Festival do Contrabando** (*cm-alcoutim.pt*), when thousands arrive to cross a temporary floating bridge complete with 'custom controllers', see smuggling reenactments, and feast on traditional dishes. South of Alcoutim, the **River Museum** (*museudealcoutim.pt; €2.90/€1.80 including the castle*), closed on Sundays and Mondays, shows smuggler interview videos and displays model river vessels.

Alcoutim's Archaeological Sites

Festival aside, Alcoutim is the Algarve's least populated town, preserving rural life. However, if you spend a few hours here, you'll soon see that its historical role isn't undersized. The 14th-century **Castelo Archaeology Museum** (*museudealcoutim.pt; €2.90/€1.80 including the River Museum*) is especially worth a visit, both for its panoramic rampart walls and to see a fascinating collection of Islamic board games excavated nearby, including from the **Old Castle of Alcoutim**, reached by a 1km uphill walk.

AN INTERNATIONAL ZIP LINE

Limite Zero's (*limitezero.com; from €25*) seasonal international zip line – the only one in the world – whooshes across the border and a time zone from Sanlúcar de Guadiana in Spain to Alcoutim at 70km/h.

See p85
for eating,
drinking and
shopping
listings

Explore
Loulé & Inland

Clinging fiercely to its heritage and serving as the de facto defender of Algarvian handicrafts, Loulé has evolved without losing its essence. A museum-like network of ancestral workshops dot the centre, cultural events run back-to-back, and at its weekly market, farmers' produce remains the protagonist rather than trinkets. Home to one of the Algarve's only standing minarets and Portugal's only (known) Islamic baths, it's equally respectful of its centuries as walled Moorish al-Ulya. In the land beyond, groves of cork trees lead to the near-silent Serra do Caldeirão range, where enduring villages and age-old traditions show little signs of wavering.

Getting Around

Walking & Cycling

Explore Loulé and the Serra do Caldeirão's villages on foot. Hiking trails and some cycling routes crisscross the countryside.

Car

With limited inland public transport, renting a car is the best way to combine scenic sights and villages in one day.

Bus

Weekday Vamus buses depart from the central station to Almancil (85), Alte and Salir (83), and São Brás de Alportel (90). Loulé Train Station is a 6km walk; the free bus connection isn't always reliable.

THE BEST

HISTORIC SIGHT Banhos Islâmicos de Loulé (p82)

HANDICRAFTS Loulé Criativo's workshops (p76)

MARKET Mercado Municipal (p83)

VILLAGE Alte (p84)

UNEXPECTED EXPERIENCE Loulé Rock Salt Mine (p83)

Mercado Municipal (p83)

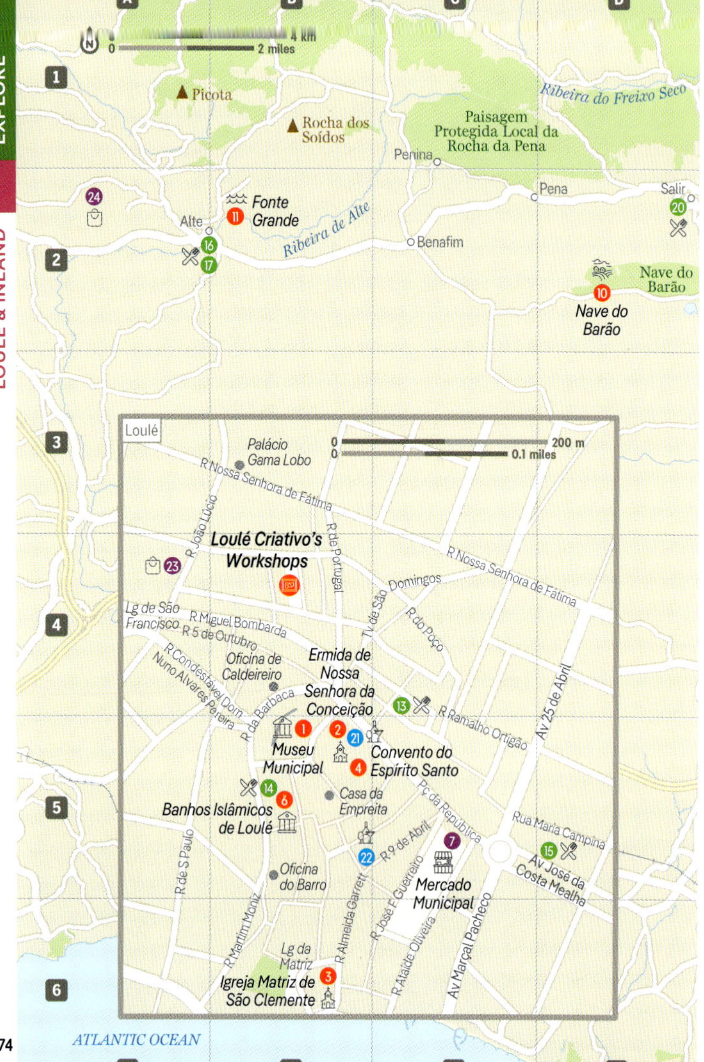
A
B
C
D
1
2
3
4
5
6
4 km
0
2 miles
Picota
Rocha dos Soídos
Paisagem Protegida Local da Rocha da Pena
Ribeira do Freixo Seco
Penina
Pena
Salir
Fonte Grande
Alte
Ribeira de Alte
Benafim
Nave do Barão
Loulé
Palácio Gama Lobo
200 m
0.1 miles
R Nossa Senhora de Fátima
R João Lúcio
Loulé Criativo's Workshops
R de Portugal
Tv de São Domingos
R do Poço
Lg de São Francisco
R Miguel Bombarda
R 5 de Outubro
Oficina de Caldeireiro
Ermida de Nossa Senhora da Conceição
R Condestável Dom Nuno Alvares Pereira
R da Barbaca
R Ramalho Ortigão
Av 25 de Abril
Museu Municipal
Convento do Espírito Santo
Casa da Empreita
Banhos Islâmicos de Loulé
Pç da República
Rua Maria Campina
Av José da Costa Mealha
R 9 de Abril
R de S Paulo
Oficina do Barro
Mercado Municipal
R Martim Moniz
R Almeida Garrett
R José F Guerreiro
R Ataíde Oliveira
Av Marçal Pacheco
Lg da Matriz
Igreja Matriz de São Clemente
ATLANTIC OCEAN

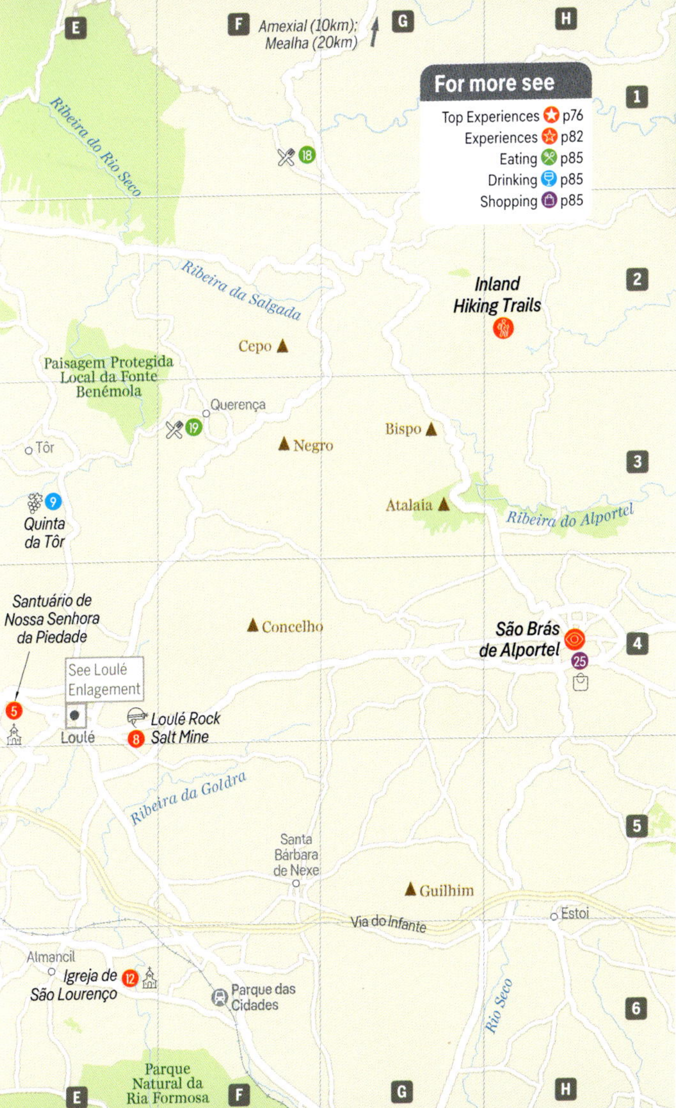
E
F
G
H
Amexial (10km);
Mealha (20km)
For more see
Top Experiences p76
Experiences p82
Eating p85
Drinking p85
Shopping p85
1
2
3
4
5
6
Ribeira do Rio Seco
18
Ribeira da Salgada
Inland
Hiking Trails
Cepo
Paisagem Protegida
Local da Fonte
Benémola
Querença
19
Tôr
Negro
Bispo
9
Quinta
da Tôr
Atalaia
Ribeira do Alportel
Santuário de
Nossa Senhora
da Piedade
Concelho
São Brás
de Alportel
25
See Loulé
Enlagement
5
Loulé
Loulé Rock
8
Salt Mine
Ribeira da Goldra
Santa
Bárbara
de Nexe
Guilhim
Via do Infante
Estoi
Almancil
Igreja de
12
São Lourenço
Parque das
Cidades
Rio Seco
Parque
Natural da
Ria Formosa

★ TOP EXPERIENCE

Loulé Criativo's Workshops

Since establishing its trade fair in 1291, Loulé has long been a leader in preserving ancestral Algarvian crafts. Across Loulé Criativo's network of six studios – linked by a walking tour – and via organised artistic workshops, their aim is preserving time-honoured techniques at risk of vanishing.

MAP: P74 **B4**

PLANNING TIPS
Visit Tuesday to Friday, as some studios (*all free entry*) close from Saturday to Monday; all shut for lunch. Educational classes and workshops require pre-booking (*loulecriativo.pt*).

Scan this QR code for workshop opening hours and to book classes.

ECOA

Start at **Palácio Gama Lobo**, ECOA's 18th-century manor-house headquarters. The acronym translates to 'Space of Knowledge, Crafts and Arts'. Here, you can request a *Rede de Oficinas* (workshops network) walking tour map, visit the temporary art exhibition, and enquire about last-minute, bookable workshops.

Workshops Around Town

In all the workshops, you'll meet working local artisans and can ask questions (language allowing). Studios double as boutiques and while purchasing is optional, all items make excellent souvenirs or gifts. The most important spaces for representing the region are the **Casa da Empreita** (Palm Weaving), demonstrating centuries-old techniques using the indigenous short palm tree; **Oficina de Caldeireiro** (Copper Workshop), to see traditional *cataplanas* (cooking pots) being hammered; and the **Oficina do Barro** (Clay Studio). The watchmaker and luthier studios (call ahead), while intricately linked with Loulé, aren't as regionally representative. The seventh studio, Casa do Esparto, weaving with local grass fibre, is in the village of **Alte** (p86).

Get Creative

Turismo Criativo's diverse workshop schedule (*from €30*) includes *azulejo* (glazed tile) painting, weaving, embroidery, cooking and typical baking. It's best to check schedules and book before arriving in the Algarve, as most require minimum numbers.

★ TOP EXPERIENCE

Inland Hiking Trails

The interior's network of trails suits any rambler. From easy loops (and cycling) in the low-lying barrocal region, with *fontes* (streams), cork trees, limestone hills and spring wildflowers, to more offbeat hikes in the Serra do Caldeirão mountain range, all encounter a more enduring Algarve.

Easy-Access Trails

The most beaten tracks are found where the barrocal meets the Serra do Caldeirão foothills. Fonte da Benémola Trail is leisurely, ambling 4.1km across streams and past old water mills in the shaded, verdant valley. More challenging, the 6.9km **PR18 LLE** around Rocha da Pena's limestone cliff (excellent rock climbing) has panoramic views and possible eagle and griffon sightings in autumn. Heading east, São Bras' 7km **PR3 SBA** (near Lajes hamlet) showcases the unwavering inland Algarve: cork trees, working donkeys, and typical stone houses.

Community Walking Festivals

Community walking festivals (*algarvewalkingseason.com*) offer informative guided hikes. The village of **Amexial** (near the Alentejo border) hosts a large event every April. From autumn to spring, the tranquil trails weaving away from the typical village (and its welcome summer pool) provide some of the region's most remote walks.

Percurso da Masmorra

The offbeat, circular, 6km **Masmorra Trail**, begins in silent Mealha village (one hour from Loulé). Taking in *palheiros* (centuries-old circular slate buildings once – and occasionally still – topped with conical thatched roofs) and the Anta da Masmorra dolmen, a 12-stone, 3rd-millennia-BCE monument, it's a remote, historic wander.

PLANNING TIPS

Tourism offices have printed maps (mobile connection can be weak), and trails are mostly marked. Summer can be unbearably hot, and refreshment stops scarce. The Via Algarviana (p82) crosses the region.

Scan this QR code for detailed trail descriptions and maps.

★ TOP EXPERIENCE

São Brás de Alportel

With a trio of museums spotlighting traditional life in the barrocal region, **São Brás de Alportel** is an excellent half-day trip. Exhibitions aside, the unhurried town is a delight to amble, be it along an ancient Roman road or to old-school cafes and original recipe *pastelarias* (pastry shops).

MAP: P75 **H4**

PLANNING TIPS
Visit Tuesday to Saturday when all museums are open. Prebook cork factory tours; if relying on public transport, Vamus 65 links São Brás with Eco-fábrica (*weekend services are limited*).

Scan this QR code to download maps and information about the town's attractions.

The Costume Museum

Housed in an *azulejo*-fronted former cork tycoon's mansion, **Museu do Traje** (*museu-sbras.com; €2.50; cash*) exhibits an impressive collection of typical Algarvian 19th- and 20th-century outfits. An audio tour, immersive elements, and contextual political and social insights support the five-figure garment collection – the majority remain in storage, visitable once a month – to tell a revealing fashion-led historical narrative. The yard and old carriage rooms are dedicated to the cork industry, displaying tools and donkey carts.

Roman Roads

Continue the walk down memory lane, quite literally, at the **Centro Explicativo da Calçadinha's** (*cm-sbras.pt; free*) small exhibit about the old Roman trade road. The main attraction is walking the weathered Roman stones yourself; one stretch of the 1480m route is accessed behind the centre.

The N2

To learn more about the country's more contemporary roads, visit the **Casa Memória EN2** (*visit saobrasalportel.pt; €2*). Exhibits inside the old road maintenance lodge, dedicated to Portugal's longest road, the north-to-south spanning N2, include tools, documentation and imagery. Information is provided

Museu do Traje
MAURO RODRIGUES/SHUTTERSTOCK ©

in Portuguese, but ask the ever-helpful Sonia to email you the digital translation document. Afterwards, consider driving the wending, viewpoint-dotted way to Amexial and the regional Alentejo border, or beyond.

Cork Factory

Cork-coated countryside surrounds São Brás de Alportel, which provided the town with much of its 19th-century wealth. Learn all about the cork harvesting and production process on an 11.30am tour at **Eco-fábrica de Cortiça** (*eco-corkfactory.com; adult/child €16.50/€8.50*), manufacturing everything from traditional wine stoppers to contemporary fashion items.

TAKE A BREAK

Pastelaria Dofir (*8am-3pm*) bakes excellent traditional cakes and serves light lunches. For a perfectly presented, high-quality dinner, make a reservation at Ysconderijo (*7-11pm Mon-Fri*).

Drive The Serra do Caldeirão's Villages

Stringing together some of the Serra do Caldeirão's rural villages and scenic viewpoints, this one-day tour is a bucolic drive. Enjoy a window into enduring Algarvian life far from the coast as you explore castle ruins, hilltop towns and pocket-sized museums. Plan for a weekday drive; most museums close on weekends.

START	END	LENGTH
Querença	Alte	49 km; 1¼ hours

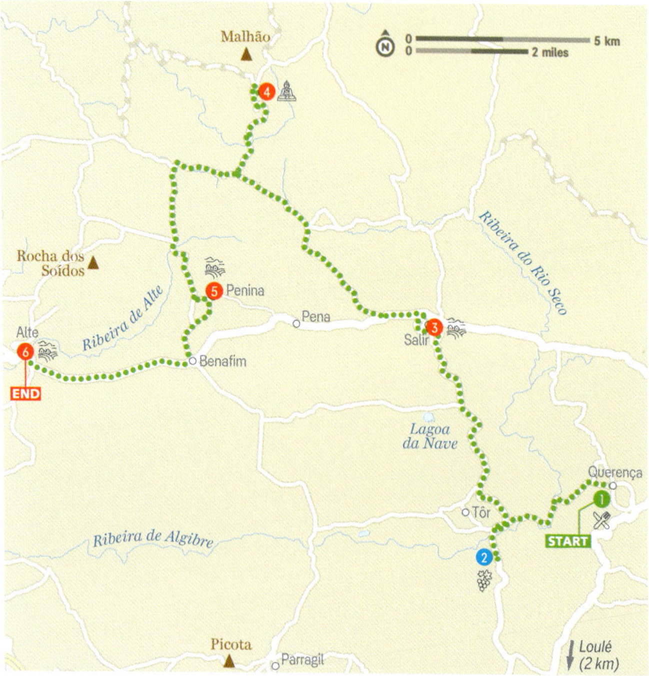

1 Pretty Church Square

Start your day with breakfast on the terrace of **Cafe D. Rosa** in Querença, an endearing hilltop village anchored around the church square. Visit the Polo Museológico da Água, a diminutive museum displaying weathered waterwheels and other equipment related to the area's historically important waterways. Museum staff hold the church's key.

2 Winery Visit

Plan to arrive at **Quinta da Tôr** before 11am for a pre-bookable tour, or swing by anytime for non-designated drivers to enjoy a tasting with vineyard views. A short drive away is the Rio Benémola and Ponte de Tôr, a reconstructed, three-arched medieval bridge. You'll recognise it as the winery's logo.

3 Castle Ruins

Continue to **Salir**, a larger, more atmospheric village perched in a pretty valley. Visit the remains of the 12th-century Moorish castle via the small Pólo Museológico de Salir (if it's closed, the ruins can be accessed via the side pathway), then stroll to the pretty church square for lunch. It's advised to park along Rua José Viegas Gregório.

4 Prayer Flag Panorama

Meandering into the mountains, passing minute hamlets and verdant scenes, the detour to the **Buddhist Stupa**, constructed in 2008, is delightful. An unexpected find, both geographically and culturally, the ridge-crowning monument has far-reaching panoramas, all the more photogenic for the fluttering prayer flags.

5 Rural Life

There's little to see in stuck-in-time **Penina**, and that's very much its appeal. The teeny village has a two-room typical rural home that acts as a museum, displaying ancestral tools and traditional homeware. Afterwards, walk the handful of narrow, whitewashed streets lined with flower pots (best avoided by car; park outside) to the community cafe.

6 Waterfall Village

End in **Alte** (p86) to see the idyllic rural village's *fontes* (streams), mills and a few artist's studios. If you've packed swimming costumes, the **Queda do Vigário** waterfall provides a refreshing dip before enjoying an early dinner with sunset views over the citrus groves. Alternatively, loop back to Loulé via **Paderne** (p96).

EXPERIENCES

See the Castle Museum's Collection
MUSEUMS

MAP: 1 P74 B5

Introduce yourself to Loulé's history at the **Museu Municipal** (*museudeloule.pt; €1.62*), closed Mondays. Partly housed inside the reconstructed Moorish castle, the ground floor (with braille panels and a ramp) focuses on locally discovered Roman and Islamic artefacts. Upstairs, one room is decorated as a traditional Algarvian kitchen. The door beyond accesses an external castle tower and the walls.

Visit Reimagined Religious Sites
CHURCHES

Loulé's churches harbour surprises. Opposite the museum, the teeny 17th-century **Ermida de Nossa Senhora da Conceição** (MAP: 2 P74 B5) is awash with blue-and-white *azulejos* But don't forget to look down; the foundations of the old Moorish wall are below the glass. **Igreja Matriz de São Clemente** (MAP: 3 P74 B6), constructed on the site of a mosque in the former medina, retains its minaret, one of the region's only examples. For culture, visit the former 17th-century **Convento do Espírito Santo** (MAP: 4 P74 B5), reborn as an undersized art gallery with a cafe in the shaded cloisters. Most unusual is the large white dome rising from a hill on the town's edge. The site of the 16th-century **Santuário de Nossa Senhora da Piedade** (MAP: 5 P74 E4), the curiously modern temple sits alongside the original, notable for its painted wooden ceiling.

Imagine the Hammam
ARCHAEOLOGICAL SITE

MAP: 6 P74 B5

Loulé's most impressive recent archaeological discovery is the **Banhos Islâmicos de Loulé** (*museudeloule.pt; free*), closed Mondays. Opened in 2022 following extensive excavations, this is the only (known) example of Islamic baths in Portugal. The modern museum constructed around the dig site isn't large, but the easy-to-digest displays and information boards help paint a picture of how the pools would have once looked.

THE VIA ALGARVIANA

This 300km, offbeat Algarve-crossing trail starts in **Alcoutim** (p71) and stays inland until ending at **Cabo de São Vicente** (p148). Split into 14 one-day sections, seven cover the Serra do Caldeirão. Sector 7, from Salir to Alte (16.4km), is a challenging but rewarding alternative to our proposed driving tour. The two stretches from Cachopo village provide the most intense and scenic experience. A helpful app (*viaalgarviana.org*) collates the trail's maps, limited accommodation (book in advance), and facilities like public showers.

Shop the Neo-Arabic Morning Market MARKET

MAP: 7 P74 C5

Opened in 1908, Loulé's **Mercado Municipal** (*Monday to Saturday*), with its arched Moorish doorways, onion-dome-topped towers, and a fluttering rainbow of fabrics, is the region's most famous and flamboyant. Fresh, local produce is always plentiful, alongside a few food-market-style restaurants in the main hall and side rooms. However, on Saturday mornings, the market is most animated, spilling onto the streets with local traders selling everything from fruit-infused honey to homemade cheeses. If you're visiting from elsewhere, it's worth waking up early as parking can be chaotic.

Descend into a Salt Mine TOUR

MAP: 8 P74 E4

Don a hard hat and enter a cage-like lift to descend 230m underground at **Loulé Rock Salt Mine** (*techsalt.pt; adult/child €25/15*) on a two-hour weekday tour. Hear the history of the explosives that created this working salt mine in 1964, study old and new machinery, and see an unexpected underground art gallery. As the salt is mainly for roads rather than human consumption, there's no tasting; for that, head to **Castro Marim** (p68).

Join Loulé's Year-Round Celebrations FESTIVALS/EVENTS

Loulé's event calendar is cultured and practically nonstop. It starts with the Algarve's largest, loudest and most colourful **carnival** in February or March (depending on Lent), which takes over the main boulevard with huge floats, dance troupes and marching bands. Over Easter proper, the solemn **Festa da Mãe Soberana** is one of Portugal's largest processions. **Festival MED**, a world music celebration, arrives in June, followed by July's **Jazz Festival**. The region-wide **Al-Mutamid Festival**, featuring Arabic music performances, also stops by. View the full annual agenda on the municipal website (*visit-loule.pt*).

Meet the Vitiners WINERY

A few wineries are near Loulé, the eastern boundary of **Lagoa's wine region** (p120). Nearest is **Quinta da Tôr** (MAP: 9 P74 E3: *quintadator.com; from €15*), a 10-minute taxi ride. Pop in anytime for a glass or tasting, or book an 11am or 2.30pm tour; the pool is especially welcome on hot days should your accommodation be without. Beyond, the teeny village of **Nave do Barão** (MAP: 10 P74 D2) hosts perhaps the region's most wholesome one-day wine festival in March or April. Major Algarvian wineries are present, but meeting the villagers and tasting their homemade, non-commercial wines, produced here since the 13th century, makes it memorable.

TRADITIONAL CELEBRATIONS

Experience the interior's traditional gastronomy, culture and customs at these locally treasured annual celebrations. In Querença, January's **Festa das Chouriças** celebrates the village's beloved blood sausages and (ironically) the patron saints of animals. São Brás de Alportel hosts one of the most unique Easter Sunday events, the **Festa das Tochas Floridas**, when flower carpets and 'torches' decorate the town. Around the same time, **Alte's Culture Week** affords ancestral custom insights, reviving fading folklore, costumes and the traditional corridinho dance, sadly rarely performed nowadays. And in July, Salir's three-day medieval festival, **Salir do Tempo**, takes the village back in time.

Explore Alte's Streets & Streams — Village

MAP: 11 P74 B2

If you've only time to visit one inland village, make it **Alte**, 30 minutes northwest of Loulé. Arguably the Algarve's most picturesque rural village, though now firmly on the tourist trail, the narrow, hill-hugging hamlet is a cluster of pretty cobbled streets and Algarve-representing street murals – including a giant Portuguese flag painted on the facing cliff. Artisanal studios include grass fibre weaving **Casa do Esparto** – part of **Loulé Criativo's workshops** (p76) – and the nearby wholesome **Fabrica de Brinquedos** (p85) toy factory. The main attractions are the waterways running through the village. On the north side, duck-fostering **Fonte Grande** passes weathered wells and a 13th-century watermill, leading to verdant trails. Near the cemetery, wooden stairs lead to the **Queda do Vigário** waterfall, a pretty, quick-refresh bathing spot. Orange groves and gorgeous scenes span outwards; walk to **Hotel Alte** for a panoramic terrace drink to relish it all, the coast glistening beyond.

Admire Almancil's Azulejo-Adorned Church — CHURCH

MAP: 12 P74 E6

Diminutive **Igreja de São Lourenço** (*diocese-algarve.pt; €2, cash*), 10 minutes south of Loulé, appears underwhelming. But beyond its unassuming exterior are floor-to-ceiling spellbinding blue-and-white *azulejos*. The work of the two master brick makers who constructed the church, the hand-painted tiles depict religious scenes, battles and events in São Lourenço's life – context provided by the included pamphlet. A highly-detailed gilded altar adds to the spectacle. Closed on Sundays and Monday mornings, and known for shutting over leisurely lunches, **Pastelaria São Lourenco** nearby is a friendly coffee and cake stop while waiting for the doors to reopen.

LISTINGS

Best Places for...

Ⓔ Budget ⒺⒺ Midrange ⒺⒺⒺ Top End

Eating

Loulé Restaurants

Bocage Ⓔ

13 C4

Dimly lit, with excellent ever-changing *pratos do dia* (daily specials), grilled fish and Iberian pork. *noon-3pm & 7-10pm Mon-Sat*

Bica Velha Ⓔ

Cave-like dining room serving mainly Algarvian wines and flavoursome small plates. *6-9pm Mon-Sat*

Pregaria Ⓔ

Portuguese sandwiches with international twists, including *bifanas* (pork) and *pregos* (beef). *noon-4pm & 6-10pm Mon-Sat*

Alte Eateries

Germano biciArte Ⓔ

Compact bike-themed cafe doubling as a cyclist pit stop with coffee, cakes and snacks alongside biking gear. *9am-7pm Thu-Tue*

O Folclore ⒺⒺ

Steaks are the standout of this lively bar-restaurant; head to the back balcony for elevated orange grove views. *9am-11pm Mon-Sat*

Serra do Caldeirão Stops

Casa dos Presuntos Ⓔ

18 F1

On the N2, this roadside cafe and bar serves freshly sliced *presunto* (dry-cured ham), hearty meals and snacks. *7am-11pm*

Cafe D. Rosa Ⓔ

19 F3

Perfect for a cold beer or light lunch looking over Querença's pretty church square. *10am-10pm*

A Villa ⒺⒺ

Excellent Salir post-hike stop with hearty, generous inland fare, including lamb stews, grilled meats and chicken piri-piri. *11am-3pm & 6.30pm-10pm Wed-Sun*

Drinking

Loulé Picks

Café Calcinha

Art-deco cafe wonderful for a classy coffee or watching occasional fado performances. *8am-11pm Tue-Sun*

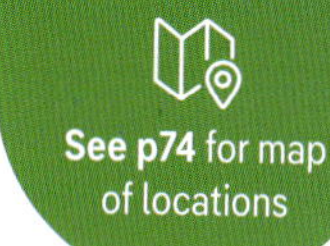
See p74 for map of locations

O Postigo

22 B5

This vivid, tiny corner bar is usually lively and overflowing, yet the wine is always poured with a smile. *11am-midnight Tue-Sat*

Shopping

Handicrafts

Projecto TASA

23 A4

Artisanal boutique with attractive ceramic and woodcraft gifts. *9.30am-5pm Mon-Fri*

Fábrica de Brinquedos

24 A2

Near Alte, this wooden-toy workshop housed in an old school is a wholesome place to shop for regional toys. *9am-noon Mon-Fri*

Centro de Artes e Ofícios

25 H4

São Brás de Alportel's tourism office has a small handicraft store where weavers are often seen at work. *9am-5pm Mon-Fri, 10am-1pm Sat & Sun*

See p98
for eating,
drinking and
shopping
listings

Explore
Albufeira & Around

In the 1960s, Albufeira seized the sun, sea and sand package holiday boom. Quickly, the traditional fishing village faded, and by 1986, its metamorphosis into a city and the Algarve's most developed beach resort was complete. But as Albufeira has reinvented itself before, following the fall of Moorish Al-Buhera and the devastating 1755 tsunami, the city is slowly evolving. New cultural hubs, boutique hotels and an underwater art gallery have arrived, while architecturally pleasing vineyards and fine-dining wine cellars provide alternatives to the (in)famous stag-party-pleasing strip. Nearby, you'll find Vilamoura Marina, Roman ruins, Salgados' birdwatching boardwalk and Armação de Pêra.

Getting Around

Walking

The old town is largely pedestrianised. An outside escalator and lift (when operational) connect viewpoints with the beach.

Bus

The main bus station (for Vilamoura, Armação de Pêra and beyond) is a 2km walk or bus connection from downtown. Albuferia's Giro buses (most have accessibility ramps) to the marina, Oura, Olhos de Água and Galé stop nearer the old town.

Train

Albufeira-Ferreiras station is 5km from downtown; there's an hourly bus connection, but it's best used for travelling longer distances.

Beach, Albufeira (p90)

UNAI HUIZI PHOTOGRAPHY/SHUTTERSTOCK ©

THE BEST

SCUBA SITE EDP Art Reef (p94)

BEACH EXPERIENCE Secluded coves by kayak (p90)

WINERY Quinta do Canhoto (p95)

BIRDING Lagos dos Salgados (p97)

MUSEUM QUARTEIRA HISTORY MUSEUM Quartiera History Museum (p96)

A
B
C
D
1
2
3
4
5
6
Albufeira
R Alves Correia
Pç Miguel Bombarda
Centro de Artes
Museu Municipal de Arqueologia
Museu de Arte Sacra
R Dr Diogo Leote
R Samora Barros
R Coronel Águas
R da Bateria
Praia dos Pescadores
ATLANTIC OCEAN
Lg do Rossio
0
400 m
0
0.2 miles
Tunes
Via do Infante
Via do Infante
Alcantarilha
Guia
Pera
Ferreiras
Ribeira de Espiche
Estrada das Ferreiras
Armação de Pêra
Fortaleza de Armação de Pêra
Lagoa dos Salgados
Praia da Galé
Praia do Evaristo
Praia do Ninho de Andorinha
Praia de São Rafael
Easy Divers
Albufeira Marina
Albufeira
See Albufeira Enlargement
EDP Art Reef
1
2
3
4
5
17
18
19
21
22
23
26
27
28
29
30
32
33

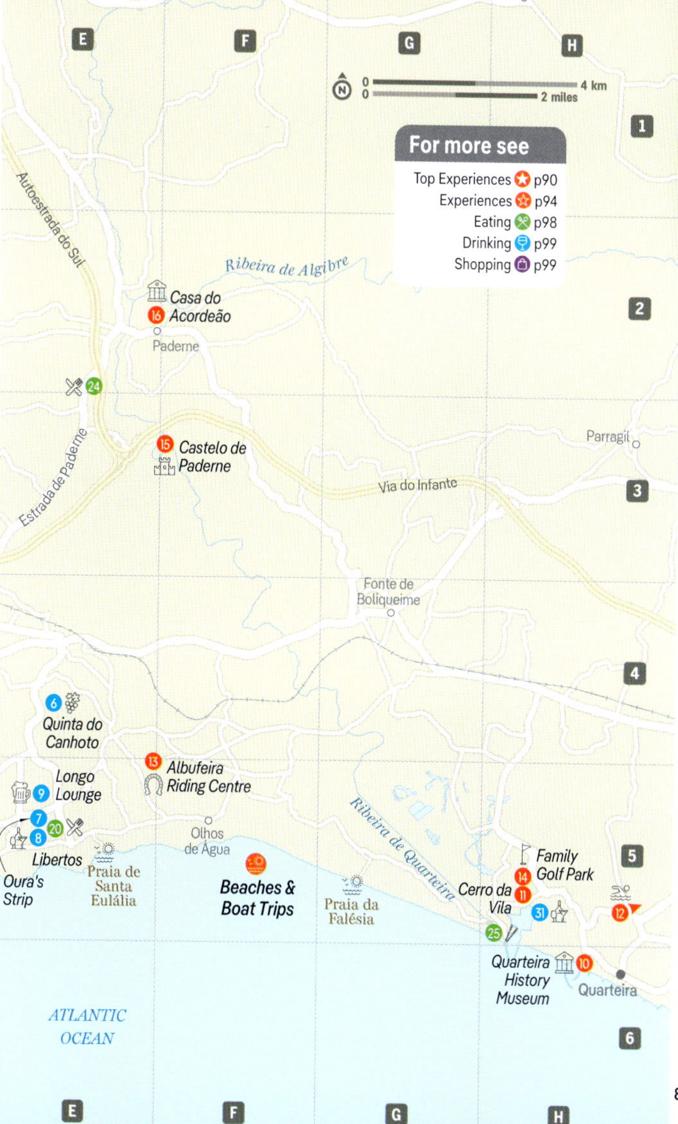

For more see
Top Experiences p90
Experiences p94
Eating p98
Drinking p99
Shopping p99
4 km
2 miles
Autoestrada do Sul
Ribeira de Algibre
Casa do Acordeão
Paderne
Castelo de Paderne
Estrada de Paderne
Via do Infante
Parragil
Fonte de Boliqueime
Quinta do Canhoto
Longo Lounge
Albufeira Riding Centre
Olhos de Água
Libertos
Oura's Strip
Praia de Santa Eulália
Beaches & Boat Trips
Praia da Falésia
Ribeira de Quarteira
Family Golf Park
Cerro da Vila
Quarteira History Museum
Quarteira
ATLANTIC OCEAN

★ TOP EXPERIENCE

Beaches & Boat Trips

Albufeira has beaches and boat trips for all. Right on the old town's doorstep are always-popular Praia do Peneco, accessed via the tunnel, and adjacent Praia dos Pescadores. Stray further for serene shorelines and less-visited craggy coves – some best explored by boat or kayak.

PLANNING TIP
Albufeira's old town beaches have lifeguards year-round unlike much of the region. Boat tours, especially to Benagil, often overrun, so keep a flexible schedule.

Scan this QR code to book SUP, surf, kayak and coasteering tours around Albufeira.

Beaches

All of Albufeira's cliff-flanked beaches are gorgeous, and many can be ambled between on rugged trails. To the east, **Praia de Santa Eulália** is a pretty but often crowded spot. For more space, drive or take the bus (Giro 6) further to **Praia da Falésia**, an accoladed 6km-long sweep of sand backed by ochre-hued cliffs that sweeps all the way to Vilamoura. Heading west, the coast is incredibly scenic around **Praia do Ninho de Andorinha**, a slightly challenging-to-access cave-like beach, and **Praia do Evaristo**, renowned for its rock formations and pools. The moderate, mainly cliff-tracking 10km (unofficial) trail between **Praia dos Arrifes** and Galé traverses some of the area's most photogenic bays. A dozen of Albufeira's beaches are deemed accessible, including **Praia dos Pescadores** and **Praia da Galé**, both with bathrooms and amphibious wheelchairs.

Water Sports

Praia da Galé (the area's main surf hub), Oura and Santa Eulália all have water-sports centres offering rentals of jet skis, pedalos, and fun rides. But a kayak rental will get you to the otherwise impossible-to-access sands west of Praia dos Arrifes. **Albufeira Surf Sup** (*albufeirasurfsup; from €35*),

Praia de São Rafael

based at **Praia de São Rafael**, offers excellent two- to three-hour group tours by kayak or SUP. They also rent kayaks (*€15/one hour*), surf and paddle boards and wetsuits.

Boat Trips

Countless boat tours depart from the candy-coloured, restaurant-packed **Albufeira Marina**, including dolphin-watching trips, boozy catamaran cruises and excursions to **Benagil Cave** (p104). **X Ride**'s (*xridealgarve.com*) smaller boats are better for exploring caves than larger vessel operators. **AlgarExperience** (*algarexperience.com*) operate some cave trips on a ramp-accessible catamaran with adapted toilets; confirm which craft is being used when booking.

LUNCH BREAK

Most beaches have a (usually pricier) snack bar. More exclusive lunch picks include Galé's Villa Joya Sea (the fusion 'little sister' to the hotel's Michelin restaurant) and Pine Cliffs' Mare.

WALKING TOUR

Walk Albufeira's Old Town

Albufeira's history may appear faded, but you'll still encounter traces on this scenic amble, taking in *miradouros* (viewpoints), Moorish memories and cultural spaces. Following a fairly pub-free route, this is the more serene side of the old town. Factor in additional time to visit the museums and galleries.

START	END	LENGTH
Albufeira Observation Deck	Miradouro do Pau da Bandeira	1.8km; 1 hour

1 Beach Views

From **Albufeira Observation Deck**, contemplate the cliffs splitting the golden sand before you in two. It's hard to imagine today, but these once-castle-topped rocks gave the city its Arabic name, Al-Buhera, meaning 'Castle on the Sea'.

2 Sacred Art

Set off in search of the relics that remain, tracking the elevated path. Pass the tiled mural depicting knights of yore towards the small **Museu de Arte Sacra**, visitable in 20 minutes.

3 Central Square

Follow the road downwards, peeping into the **Centro de Artes** teeny exhibition before arriving at **Jardim Público de Albufeira**, the old town's main square. Pay a brief visit to **Galeria de Arte Pintor Samora Barros**, named in honour of a local artist, where there's usually a free, temporary Albufeira-linked art exhibition, plus public toilets.

4 Historic Finds

Walk towards the Albufeira Tunnel, framing the beach beyond. But rather than heading for the shoreline, climb the stairs to see the small clutch of archaeological discoveries inside the **Museu Municipal de Arqueologia**. In front, a circled area spotlights the remains of low Moorish-built house walls, part of the former castle. Detour down **Rua Henrique Calado** to see the only real remains of the castle's wall exposed on the far corner.

5 Shells & Seafood

Returning to the ocean-facing path, once the former castle's front, continue towards the shell-adorned **Porta de Sant Ana**, one of three former gates, mostly destroyed in the 1755 earthquake. Nowadays, the small Portas Da Villa Antiquity Bar occupies the space. After a refreshing drink, turn right at the bottom of the stairs towards **Cais Herculano**, an open-sided building that served as the city's seafood market when the beach was a fishing hub.

6 Pretty Panorama

After pausing at the fishermen-dedicated **Monumento ao Pescador** and trying to picture pre-tourism Praia dos Pescadores, dotted with colourful boats rather than beach towels, take the outside escalator to **Miradouro do Pau da Bandeira**. Perhaps now, if you squint, you'll imagine that castle.

EXPERIENCES

Learn Albufeira's History

MUSEUMS

History and culture come in bite-size portions at Albufeira's two main museums. Igreja de São Sebastião houses the **Museu de Arte Sacra** (MAP: 1 P88 **B2**; *adult/child €3/€2*), closed on Wednesdays. The exhibit includes a small set of 16th-century hand-painted religious *azulejos* (glazed tiles), gold embroidered 20th-century church garments, and a striking blue jade altar. The **Museu Municipal de Arqueologia** (MAP: 2 P88 **C2**), closed on Mondays, begins with an informative timeline projection of the local area. The rest of the two-floor space (with tactile flooring and a lift) displays archaeological discoveries spanning prehistory until today, including a Roman mosaic and part of an Islamic silo.

See Submerged Art

SCUBA DIVING

Whether you're certified or looking for a first-time dive experience, there are two reasons to submerge yourself in Albufeira: Portugal's largest natural reef and the **EDP Art Reef** (MAP: 3 P88 **D6**) sunk in 2023. Containing sculptures fashioned from a decommissioned power station, the work by Portuguese street artist Vhils is Albufeira's newest artificial reef – shallow enough to be seen on a first-time afternoon discovery dive. Marina-based **Easy Divers** (MAP: 4 P88 **D5**; *easydivers.pt; €100*) provide introductory classes in their inside training pool before everyone lugs their tanks to their spacious boat and heads for the waters. It's a professional and long-standing outfit, with one instructor per pair of learners and extra attention is paid to ensure children enjoy the experience.

REGIONAL SEAFOOD RECIPES

Bacalhau (salted codfish) is Portugal's national obsession, though cod isn't caught locally; it mainly arrives from Norway. For truly local seafood specialities, try Olhão's clam version of *xerém de conquilhas*, a Moorish-influenced corn-flour dish comparable to porridge; *conquilhas à Algarvia*, small clams pulled from the sand at low tide, cooked with garlic, coriander, lemon, and oil; and *muxama*, a Moorish-era salt-cured tuna speciality. From April until October, *sardinhas assadas* (charcoal grilled sardines) become a much-loved staple, especially during summer celebrations. *Arroz de marisco* (seafood rice stews) are plentiful, though the Algarve's *de lingueirão* (razor clam version) arguably takes top billing.

When booking, confirm the dive site schedule if you're committed to the art reef, keeping in mind ocean conditions on the day dictate the final decision.

Take a Creative Workshop

HANDICRAFTS

MAP: 5 P88 B1

Repurposed from the city's former courthouse in 2023, the **Centro de Artes** *(cm-albufeira.pt)*, closed on Sundays, aims to bring Algarvian artistic heritage back to the old town. Inside, there's a small temporary exhibition space and shelves selling handcrafted wares from local artisans. Anna, on the desk, is always happy to explain the heritage of the craft methods used. Throughout the year, the centre hosts various workshops, ranging from one-day ceramic classes to multiday weaving lessons; check schedules online and book in advance.

Tour Urban Vines

WINERY

MAP: 6 P88 E4

Quinta do Canhoto *(quintadocanhoto.com; from €25)*, a 15-minute taxi ride from the old town, is a true family affair – even the striking, white-lined, bioclimatic building was designed by a family member. Better still for parents, families are especially welcome in summer when the team hosts kids' painting activities so parents can fully appreciate their tour and tasting. Tours through the vines are held on weekdays, ending with tasting four wines. Visiting for a picnic amongst the vines is also possible, but as with the tours, they require reservations.

BEST ACTIVITIES WITH KIDS

Aquashow

MAP: 12 P89 H5

Quarteira's colossal water park has rides, slides and a year-round indoor area *(aquashowpark.com; adult/junior €33/24)*.

Albufeira Riding Centre

MAP: 13 P89 E5

Over sixes can join the Saturday morning Pony Club *(albufeiraridingcentre.com; €30)*.

Family Golf Park

MAP: 14 P89 H5

Choose from two themed 18-hole mini golf courses in Vilamoura *(familygolfpark.pt; from €11)*.

Party on Oura's Infamous Strip

NIGHTLIFE

Brash, neon-blazing, and not for everyone, **Oura's Strip** (MAP: 7 P88 E5) is Albufeira's infamous road where beers flow freely. Amongst the lively, packed bars, there are some calmer corners such as **Connection** (see 7 P88 E5), Albufeira's main LGBTIQ+ venue on a first-floor balcony, **Libertos'** (MAP: 8 P88 E5) tree-shaded cocktail garden (early evening), and nearby **Longo Lounge** (MAP: 9 P88 **E5**), offering a more local and relaxed vibe.

Visualise History in Vilamoura & Quarteira

MUSEUMS

Side by side, Vilamoura, the country's largest marina and a luxury coastal resort, and the city of Quarteira, are opposites – but they share history. The informative **Quarteira History Museum** (MAP: 10 P88 H6; *free*), closed on Mondays, dives deep into the area's previous 6000 years, displaying archaeological finds... but more interestingly, a narrative from the local community about long-lost fishing huts and Vilamoura's construction. Behind the splashy marina, the area's original lavish villa is the Roman archaeological site of **Cerro da Vila** (MAP: 11 P88 **H5**; *vilamouraworld.com; adult/child €4/€2*), though just the base walls and some mosaics remain.

Visit Paderne Village & Castle

HERITAGE

Paderne, 20 minutes inland from Albufeira, feels a world away. Visit to see the **Castelo de Paderne** (MAP: 15 P88 **F3**), a 12th-century Moorish rammed-earth fortification and one of the seven castles depicted on the Portuguese flag. Although usually closed – Albufeira's tourist office arranges occasional Wednesday tours – there's a 3km looped trail linking the castle, a ruined three-arched medieval bridge and an old communal bread oven. A QR code outside the castle downloads an audio guide. The village's **Casa do Acordeão** (MAP: 16 P89 E2), closed weekends, is dedicated to the accordion, the Algarve's most typical 19th-century folk instrument.

Go Bird Watching

BOARDWALK

MAP: 17 P88 **B5**

Beyond Albufeira's craggy coves, Praia Grande de Pêra is an almost endless swathe of sand. Backed by

GUIA, THE 'PIRI-PIRI CHICKEN CAPITAL'

The Algarve's famed fiery dish has a story steeped in colonising history. During the Age of Discovery, bird's-eye chillies were transported from South America and then grown in the Portuguese colonies of Cabo Verde and Mozambique, where the spicy sauce is believed to have first appeared. In the 1970s, as Portuguese settlers returned from these colonies, the chillies were infused with more European ingredients, such as garlic, olive oil and lemon. *Churrasqueiras* (grill restaurants) are the best place to sample this spatchcocked charcoal-grilled chicken, especially in Guia where **Restaurante Ramires** is considered to have established the recipe.

Avocet, Lagoa dos Salgados
NEIL BOWMAN/SHUTTERSTOCK ©

Lagoa dos Salgados' freshwater wetlands, this is one of the region's vital birdlife havens. Depending on the season, flamingos, terns, warblers, weavers and many rarely seen birds can be sighted from viewing platforms along an extensive, flat boardwalk.

Splash around Armação de Pêra BEACH TOWN

MAP: 18 P88 **A5**

In 2024, a foot bridge across the Ribeira de Alcantarilha was inaugurated, linking serene Salgados with busy Armação de Pêra. A popular beach resort with locals, Armação de Pêra is worth visiting for excellent and fair-priced restaurants, a beach day, or to see the historic **Fortaleza de Armação de Pêra**. Beyond, **Capela de Nossa Senhora da Rocha** (p104) is one of the Algarve's prettiest viewpoints.

LISTINGS

Best Places for...

€ Budget €€ Midrange €€€ Top End

Eating

Brunch & Bites

20age €

19 D4

Near Albufeira train station, the extensive and excellent *petiscos* (small plates) menu allows for a sampling of all Portugal's flavours. *11am-11pm Thu-Mon*

Al-Gharb Coffee Roasters €

20 E5

Sunny, spacious courtyard for barista-quality, own-roasted coffee and international-style brunches. *9am-4pm*

Iguana Cafe €

21 B2

Breakfasts, burgers and salads on a show-stealing beach-view terrace overlooking Albufeira's old town. *noon-7pm*

Local Flavours

Solgamba €

22 B2

Reliable, authentic Algarvian specialities such as *cataplana* (seafood stew), chicken piri-piri, and seafood kebabs. *noon-10pm Tue-Sun*

Casa da Fonte €€

23 B2

Long-standing restaurant for traditional dishes across various dining areas, including a cute fountain-soundtracked courtyard. *noon-11pm*

Reservation-Worthy Restaurants

Veneza €€

24 E2

Near Paderne, dishes here are (almost) secondary to one of Portugal's best wine cellars embellishing every wall. *7-10pm Wed-Mon, noon-2.30pm Fri & Sun*

Thai Beach Club €€

25 H5

Cross the Vilamoura Marina bridge to this funky beachside Thai restaurant with occasional sunset DJ parties. *11am-11pm*

Windmill €€€

26 A1

This windmill built in 1938 is now a romantic adult-only restaurant serving three-course Mediterranean menus. *6.30-10pm*

A Sardinha €€€

27 C5

Praia dos Arrifes's beach restaurant brags sensational seafood (mainly priced by weight) and stupendous rock-formation views. *11am-9pm*

Armação de Pêra Eats

Inevitável Wine Bar €€

28 A4

Exemplary traditional dishes like *muxama* (cured tuna) and *xerém* (corn-based porridge) with first-class, informative service, wine pairings and vegetarian options. *4-10pm Fri-Wed*

Olivalmar €€€

29 A5

One of the Algarve's best *marisqueiras* (seafood

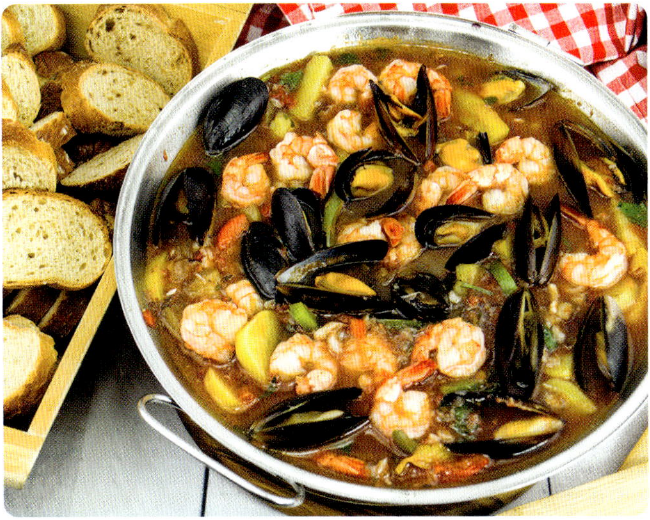

Cataplana

restaurants) serving heaped shellfish and mollusc platters against lapping-wave views. *noon-10pm*

Drinking

Wine & Cocktails

Café In-certo

 B1

Peaceful old town tapas bar serving flawless sangria and local beers with sharing boards and light bites available. *9am-midnight Mon-Sat*

Atlantic Piano Bar

 H5

Overlooking Vilamoura Marina, this lively, trendy terrace has quality cocktails and regular live music. *4pm-2am*

Shopping

Handicrafts & Markets

Pau de Pita

 B1

Arguably, Albufeira's best gifts shop is one of the few that sell typical and local (rather than mass-produced) pottery and textiles. *10am-6pm*

Mercado Municipal dos Caliços

 D5

Away from the old town, Albufeira's semi-outdoors market provides a more authentic taste of city life with chatty traders and farm-fresh produce. *8am-2pm Tue-Sat*

See p112
for eating, drinking and shopping listings

Explore Lagoa & Portimão

Flanking either side of the Arade's estuary, the neighbouring municipalities of Lagoa and Portimão boast some of the Algarve's most celebrated craggy coastline. Encompassing award-winning Praia da Marinha and festival-hosting Praia da Rocha, breathtaking but crowded Benagil Cave, excellent shipwreck diving, and the cliff-topping Seven Hanging Valleys Trail, the shoreline steals the spotlight. Pretty whitewashed fishing villages, including Alvor, Carvoeiro, and Ferragudo, all add to the low-rise seaside charm. Away from the beach, laid-back Lagoa and sardine-obsessed Portimão, the Algarve's second city, provide a more local and lived-in experience, with vineyards, an excellent waterpark, pottery workshops and flamingo sightings nearby.

Getting Around

Bus

Vamus buses connect Portimão with Lagoa, Carvoeiro (107), and Ferragudo (110). The summer-only 52 provides additional coastal connections. Portimao's local bus station is central; the intercity terminal is near the arena. Use Vai e Vem buses for Praia da Rocha and Alvor.

Boat

A water taxi bridges Ferragudo with Portimão.

Trains

Portimão's station is fairly central; Estômbar-Lagoa and Ferragudo are less helpfully located. Carvoeiro and Ferragudo have a seasonal wheeled 'tourist train'.

Algar de Benagil (p104)

THE BEST

COASTAL TRAIL Percurso dos Sete Vales Suspensos (p104)

MUSEUM Museu de Portimão (p108)

ARTS & CRAFTS Azulejo Painting Workshop (p108)

SEA CAVES Zip&Trip (p111)

WINERY Quinta dos Santos (p109)

A
B
C
D
1
2
3
4
5
6
N125
Via do Infante
Ribeira de Boina
Skydive Algarve
Aeródromo Municipal de Portimão
Estrada de Montes de Alvor
Portimão
Rio Arade
R Infante Dom Henrique
R Infante de Sagres
Conserveira do Arade
Golf Land
Estrada de Alvor
Portimão
Ria de Alvor
Av São Lourenço da Barrosa (V6)
Rio Arade
Ria de Alvor Nature Reserve
Variante 3
Variante 8
Zip&Trip
See Portimão Enlargement
Portimão
0 1 km
0 0.5 miles
R de Olivença
Ponte Velha de Portimão
R Direita
Av Guanaré
Av Miguel Bombarda
Portisub
Museu de Portimão
Rio Arade
Estrada da Rocha
Ferragudo
Arti Arte Azulejar
Av das Comunidades Lusíadas
Av Tomás Cabreira
Av Rio Arade
Praia da Rocha
Algarve SunBoat
NoSoloÁgua

E F G H

1

Via do Infante

Quinta dos Vales 4

28

Estômbar-Lagoa

Slide & Splash 12

26

Lagoa

2

43

N125

Via do Infante

Olaria Pequena 10

Monte de Salicos 5

SandCity 13

Porches Pottery 9

37

Quinta dos Santos 3

Estrada das Sesmarias

3

Estrada do Carvoeiro

Estrada da Caramujeira

25

24

35

Carvoeiro

22

21

23

36

Carvoeiro Caves

Vale de Centeanes

Percurso dos Sete Vales Suspensos

Estrada de Benagil

Clear Emotions

Capela de Nossa Senhora da Rocha

Praia da Marinha

Algar de Benagil

Carvoeiro's Coastal Trails

4

ATLANTIC OCEAN

For more see

Top Experiences p104
Experiences p108
Eating p112
Drinking p113
Shopping p113

5

6

0 — 4 km
0 — 2 miles

E F G H

★ TOP EXPERIENCE

Carvoeiro's Craggy Coastline

One of the Algarve's original holiday darlings, Carvoeiro outgrew its fishing village origins while retaining copious charm. With a full deck of coastal credentials – cliff-topping boardwalk, craggy rock pools and breathtaking caves – plus the beach-hopping Seven Hanging Valleys Trail nearby, its coastline is cinema-worthy.

MAP P102 **G4**

TRAIL EXTENSIONS
Beyond Marinha, a less trodden path continues to **Capela de Nossa Senhora da Rocha**, a photogenic chapel atop a beach-splitting headland. The 6km Caminho dos Promontórios links Carvoeiro and Ferragudo.

Scan this QR code to access a downloadable trail plan.

Algar Seco & Carvoeiro Boardwalk

The short, step-free, cliff-topping **Carvoeiro Boardwalk** brags impeccable ocean views, with the rock-carved staircase leading to Algar Seco's natural pools. Shuffle behind them and scramble up rocks for more impressive vistas before heading behind rock-wedged **Restaurante Boneca Bar** to see the cave's window framing the ocean. It's possible to extend the main trail by following the cliffs from the car park.

Percurso dos Sete Vales Suspensos

Linking **Vale de Centeanes** and **Praia da Marinha**'s jaw-dropping rock formations, the moderate, marked 6km **Percurso dos Sete Vales Suspensos** route climbs and descends rugged terrain cliffs between gorgeous golden sand beaches. Along the way, see Farol de Alfanzina lighthouse, pause at pine-shaded picnic areas and peek into fenced sinkholes and caves – including Algar de Benagil, which can be visited en route. Plan two hours minimum (plus swimming time) for a one-way hike.

Benagil Cave

A victim of its own beauty, the natural skylight-illuminated beach of **Algar de Benagil** has become congested and controversy-prone. Briefly closed due

Praia da Marinha

JUAMPITER/GETTY IMAGES ©

to erosion and crowding concerns, authorities implemented new visiting regulations in August 2024, prohibiting swimming to the cave and unguided kayak visits/rentals, and banning landing on the grotto's beach; fines are in place for non-compliance. Licensed, guided SUP or kayak tour operators, such as Benagil-based **Clear Emotions** (*clearemotions.pt; from €25*), can take you for an eight-minute interior peek, while boat tours are limited to two minutes inside. This can lead to long on-water waits in summer; try to book the day's first trip. Thankfully, Benagil is far from being the only cave along this stretch of coast, and tours then continue to other nearby grottos. As the area and parking often become crowded, consider boat trips from further afield; **Carvoeiro Caves** (*carvoeirocaves.com; from €25*) depart from Praia do Carvoeiro.

PLANNING TIPS

Cliff trails are unguarded; wear suitable walking shoes. Sunrise is best for breezy, golden light and calmer scenes around **Benagil**, though **Marinha**'s sunsets are undeniably spectacular. Bring plenty of water.

Walk Portimão & Praia da Rocha

High-rise Portimão is one of the region's most wheelchair-friendly destinations thanks to the 6km Rota Acessível, a dedicated mural-adorned pathway. This mainly step-free tour traces part of the route, exploring the city's heritage, street art and former sardine canning industry before ending coastal.

START	END	LENGTH
Praça da República	Praia da Rocha	3.6km; 1½ hours

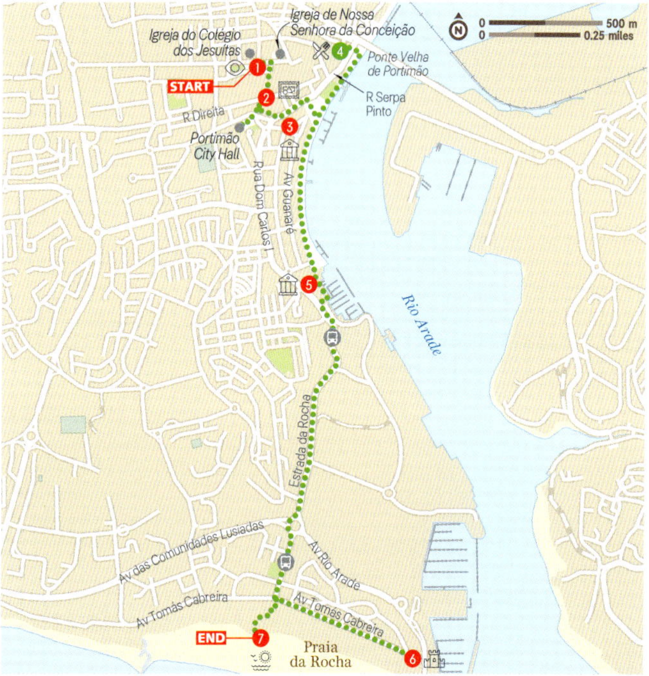

Igreja de Nossa Senhora da Conceição
Igreja do Colégio dos Jesuítas
START
Ponte Velha de Portimão
R Serpa Pinto
R Direita
Portimão City Hall
Rua Dom Carlos I
Av Guanaré
Rio Arade
Estrada da Rocha
Av das Comunidades Lusíadas
Av Rio Arade
Av Tomás Cabreira
END
Praia da Rocha
500 m
0.25 miles

1 Historic Square

Start the marked trail at **Praca da República**, dominated by the 17th-century **Igreja do Colégio dos Jesuítas** (inaccessible). Nearby, the Gothic **Igreja de Nossa Senhora da Conceição**, extensively reconstructed following the 1755 earthquake, has a steep side ramp and a small entrance-door bump.

2 Street Art & Shops

Follow the path into the downtown **shopping area**, passing sardine murals and colourful tile-fronted buildings before detouring to see the baroque **Palácio Bivar**, now the City Hall. A mural of Portugal's most famed footballer, Cristiano Ronaldo, looks on.

3 Miniature Museum

The graffiti-coated section of the trail passes **Casa Manuel Teixeira Gomes**, a museum inside the former President's home. The courtyard has a small step; exhibitions aren't accessible. Opposite, see the leafy garden (off the path, but there's lowered curb access) fronting the 18th-century theatre.

4 Seafood Stop

At Ribeirinha waterfront square (NoSolo Italia cafe has an accessible toilet), the dedicated path turns right. However, a secondary bike trail leads left (the waterfront is flat with polished cobbles), passing gardens and the ramp-accessible tourism office, which occasionally hosts exhibitions. A tunnel behind leads to **sardine grilling restaurants**; Peixarada has a ramp.

5 Sardine Stories

Retrace your route south towards the **Museu de Portimão**. You'll spot tall brick chimneys on the horizon, denoting former canning factories, and a collection of stone sculptures approaching the museum. Housed inside a renovated former sardine factory, it is informative, interactive and fully accessible, with ramps and lifts to the lower floor.

6 Fortress Panorama

Take the bus (11/33; with ramps) from behind the museum to 16th-century **Fortaleza de Santa Catarina**. The fortress (small entrance bump) provides sweeping views of Praia da Rocha.

7 Beach Break

Praia da Rocha is a designated accessible beach. However, the road sloping down to the sands (behind the Tourism Office) is steep. Follow the beach boardwalk right to post six, with a ramp to the sand-slicing boardwalk. Praia do Vau (1P bus) has better access and seasonal amphibious wheelchairs at the lifeguard station.

EXPERIENCES

Paint an Azulejo in Ferragudo

WORKSHOP

Unlike most former fishing villages, **Ferragudo** (MAP: 1 P102 **C5**) has kept its small harbour alive. Nets, baskets and colourful fishing boats still feed the daily fish market and waterfront restaurants. It's an art-inspiring backdrop, especially when paired with the private-castle-crowned public beach and a stroll around the pretty bougainvillaea-shaded streets – so where better to master the craft of hand-painting azulejos? At **Arti Arte Azulejar's** (MAP: 2 P102 **C5**; *arti-arte-azulejar.pt; €35*) three-hour workshops, Carla will impart her *azulejo* knowledge while guiding you through painting your own design. Due to the three- to five-day turnaround for tile glazing, classes are best prebooked at the start of your trip.

Tour a Conserveira

CANNING FACTORY

MAP: 6 P102 **D2**

Towering red-brick chimneys topped with stork nests speckle the skyline on either side of the Rio Arade, pinpointing former canning factories. These were the estuary's economic lifeblood for centuries until the final factory closed in 1994. Twenty-ish years later, inspired by Portimão's sardine-focused museum, Belgium-born Vincent teamed up with Portuguese Miguel to revive the local canning industry, opening **Conserveira do Arade** (*conserveiradoarade.com; adult/under 12s €10/free*). On one-hour weekday morning tours, Elisa and the team explain the process, including cleaning, cooking, canning and labelling, before an artisan fish-produce tasting.

Study Portimão's Sardine Story

MUSEUM

MAP: 7 P102 **B4**

Much of Portimão's growth came from the sardine canning industry that thrived for around a century from 1890. For an informative overview, spend an hour in the fully accessible **Museu de Portimão** (*museudeportimao.pt; €3; closed on Mondays*). Start your visit outside by the pier's string of woven baskets where the daily catch was dumped before alarms rang out to alert the factory workers of its arrival. The baskets were used to transport fish into the now-converted *conserveira* (canning factory). Inside the modern space, exhibitions of tools, canning labels, and video interviews tell the sardine city's story. The second hall retains many original features, including the extended fish-washing sinks with human-size statues 'working' on the fishing process.

Visit the Alcalar Megalithic Site

PREHISTORY

MAP: 8 P102 **A1**

A small section of the Museu de Portimão displays artefacts

from the 5000-year-old village of Alcalar's tombs and circular stone buildings. However, visiting the **Alcalar Megalithic Site** funerary monument itself, a 20-minute drive from Portimão, is a more immersive way to appreciate Portimão's prehistory. Open from Tuesday to Saturday, the monument can be accessed with a combined museum or individual (€2) ticket.

Shop Pottery in Porches STUDIOS

Clay has been an integral part of Algarvian history for millennia. However, the arrival of the Romans and, later, the Moors elevated it to an art form. Some of the Algarve's best modern producers are based in Porches. At long-established and renowned **Porches Pottery** (MAP: 9 P102 **G2**), witness artisans at work painting glazed bowls and terracotta plates before shopping their signature designs. Nearby, **Olaria Pequena** (MAP: 10 P102 **H2**) produces more contemporary pieces.

Sail the Arade River BOAT EXCURSION

The Rio Arade was an important trade route from Phoenician times, shuttling wares upstream to Silves. The river is only navigable by smaller boats at high tides. **Algarve SunBoat**'s (MAP: 11 P102 **B6**; *algarvesunboat.com; adult/child €36/€23*) near-silent solar-powered tours depart from Portimão Marina, with skipper António pointing out Portimão's cannery chimneys, a crevice-hidden fishermen's chapel and the vineyards en route. **Ferragudo Boat Trips** (see 1; *ferragudoboattrips.com; €40*), captained by Luis onboard a traditional Algarvian fishing boat, offers Ferragudo departures. Both spend around 90 to 120 minutes in Silves – enough

BEST WINERIES

Quinta dos Santos

MAP: 3 P102 **E3**

Book tastings and tours of this gorgeously renovated winery or dine in the vine-facing restaurants. Co-owner Greg brews the local Dos Santos beers (*quintadossantos.com; from €45; Tuesday to Saturday*).

Quinta dos Vales

MAP: 4 P102 **E1**

Open-air art decorates the vines of this upscale winery, open for afternoon tours and tastings. A more expensive winemaker experience teaches you how to blend, bottle, label and cork your own personalised wine (*quintadosvales.pt; from €36*).

Monte de Salicos

MAP: 5 P102 **F2**

Carvoeiro's closest vineyard is low-key and intimate, offering personable tastings and catered dining in the vines (*montedesalicos@gmail.com; from €15*).

BEST ACTIVITIES WITH KIDS

Slide & Splash

MAP: 12 P102 **E2**

With abundant slides for kids and teens, pools, and a themed play area, this long-established waterpark is a winner. (*slidesplash.com; adult/child €27/€20/online discount*).

SandCity

MAP: 13 P102 **G2**

Off the N125, this open-air attraction displays huge sand sculptures of celebrities and landmarks (*sandcity.pt; adult/child €9.50/€4.70*).

Golf Land

MAP: 14 P102 **A2**

Alvor's family-friendly 18 hole mini golf course has tropical plants and walkable cascades, though there's little shade (*golfland.pt; adult/child €12/€7*).

time to visit the Castelo de Silves (p124) – before returning.

Spot Dolphins — BOAT TRIP

see 1

For a better chance of seeing cetaceans than on a cave tour, book a two-hour dedicated excursion with **Wildwatch** (*wildwatch.pt; adult/child €45/30*) from Ferragudo. The marine biologist team are so confident about dolphins sightings that they guarantee a complimentary second trip if the first is unsuccessful.

Scuba Inside Shipwrecks — DIVING

MAP: 15 P102 **B4**

The **Ocean Revival Project**, an artificial reef formed of four Portuguese Navy vessels, was sunk off the Portimão coast in 2012. Ranging from 44m to 102m in length, wreck divers will relish exploring the ships' interiors, while non-divers can 'experience' the project in the submarine-style cistern room at Museu de Portimão. Local diving club **Portisub** (*facebook.com/portisub; prices vary*) can help arrange visits.

Beeline to the (Beach) Club — ENTERTAINMENT

Of all the Algarve's beach clubs, **NoSoloÁgua** (MAP: 16 P102 **B6**; 11am to 7pm) is the crowd-pleaser. There's an ocean-facing pool bar (adult-only at weekends) and a separate, terraced restaurant with beach cabanas overlooking the water's teen-friendly inflatable slides and play area. In summer, sunset sessions and occasional DJ parties are hosted. After dark, the party continues along **Praia da Rocha**'s clifftop (MAP: 17 P102 **B6**), lined with late-night pubs and clubs.

Snorkel Quite Caves — WATER SPORTS

Around Alvor's **Praia de Boião**, cliff-backed bays, grottos and inaccessible beaches continue. While you could attempt to snorkel here alone, it's safer to tackle the narrow and almost missable caves with a guide. Inês and Pedro, marine biologists and founders of **Zip&Trip** (MAP: 18 P102 **B3**; *zipandtripalgarve.com; adult/child €60/€20*), know this crevice-crammed stretch inside out. Their half-day grotto snorkelling tours also help preserve ecosystems frequently disturbed by boats. While none are as cavernous as Benagil, it's a much less trafficked grotto alternative. To explore east of the Arade's estuary, join Ferragudo-based **Algarve Freedom Kayaks**' (see 1; *algarvefreedomkayaks.pt; €30*) active but rewarding four-hour kayak tours.

See Alvor's Flamingos

NATURE RESERVE

MAP: 19 P102 **A2**

Behind Alvor's sweeping dune-backed beach, the **Ria de Alvor Nature Reserve** teems with birdlife, including black-winged stilts and Caspian terns. One of the Algarve's longest boardwalks, the **Passadiços de Alvor,** circles the estuary, providing a pleasant pre-beach amble with birdwatching viewpoints. It's especially magical between November and March when a flamboyance of flamingos often flies above. An oyster farm, **OstraSelect** (p139), operates on the estuary's far side.

Sky Dive Above Alvor

SKYDIVING

MAP: 20 P102 **A1**

For a spectacular free-fall view of the Algarve's glimmering coastline, take flight with **Skydive Algarve** (*skydivealgarve.com; from €139*) from Portimão Aerodrome. Offering tandem parachute jumps from 7500ft to 15,000ft, with upgrade options to arrange a landing directly on Alvor beach, the reassuring team has been based here for a decade. **Sevenair** (*flysevenair.com*) also offers scenic Algarve flights and scheduled twin-prop departures to regional airports including Cascais and Bragança from the aerodrome.

LOCAL FESTIVALS & EVENTS

Carvoeiro hosts the Algarve's biggest start-of-summer-party in June when **Black and White Night** (outfits) sees more than 30,000 people pack the streets and beaches for dancing and drinks. In late July, Portimão's legendary **Sardine Festival** (*festivaldasardinha.pt*) takes over the waterfront with sardine-grilling and big-name Portuguese performers. Lagoa's locally loved FATACIL, with artisanal products, regional food stalls and live music, follows in August. Praia da Rocha hosts major international music festivals, including Afro Nation, throughout the summer. Year-round, the two municipalities organise many excellent and free cultural events; check agendas at *welcometolagoa.pt* and *visitportimao.com*.

LISTINGS

Best Places for...

See p102 for map of locations

€ Budget €€ Midrange €€€ Top End

Eating

Carvoeiro Picks

Tapas da Vila €
21 E4
Come for beach views, plump garlic prawns and jugs of sparkling sangria on the teeny terrace. *noon-9.30pm Thu-Tue*

Casa Algarvia €€
22 F3
Long-standing restaurant serving traditional dishes and catch of the day at fair prices in a homely dining room. *noon-10pm*

Earth Café €€
23 F4
Healthy brunches, fusion dishes and fresh juices make this a breakfast go-to; the bench seating has sea views. *8.30am-4pm Wed-Mon*

The Square €€€
24 E3
Respected local chef Raquel Marques' venture in Monte Carvoeiro focuses on fine-dining dishes; there's also a mimosa brunch menu. *10am-3pm & 6pm-1am Sun-Fri*

Lagoa Favourites

Chicken George €
25 F3
Eating chicken piri-piri here feels like dining in a family lounge. It's an unfussy, homely, shared-table affair that harks back to the Algarve of old. *6-10pm*

Gaspacho & Migas €€
26 F2
This contemporary restaurant serves creative takes on Mediterranean dishes with knowledgeable service and an interesting wine list. *6.30-10pm Mon-Sat*

O Velho Novo €€
27 C5
Ferragudo has no shortage of waterfront fish restaurants, but this local spot delivers more wallet-friendly Portuguese dishes in a dark-wood decorated dining room. *5.30-11pm Mon-Sat*

O Charneco €€€

28 E1
Fixed price, no menu, adorable family-run restaurant offering eight-course Algarvian tastings, including wine, for under €40 in Estômbar. *6.30-10pm Mon-Sat*

Portimão Cafes

Casa da Isabel €
29 B4
The glass cabinet at this old-school, tiled cafe is packed with delicious cakes, including *pastel de nata* and regional specialities, 9am-7pm Thu-Tue

Pastelaria Snack Ruby €
30 B4
Cosy cafe with friendly owners serving all the staples. It's particularly known for its *francesinhas*, Porto's meat-heavy, gravy-soaked sandwiches. *8am-7pm Mon-Fri*

Portimão Restaurants

Dona Barca €
31 B4
An institutional seafood restaurant famed for its grilled sardines. *noon-3pm & 6-9.30pm Wed-Mon*

AllGarbe €€

32 B4
One of Portimão's premier and most popular modern seafood restaurants, with fish and oysters on ice, and a local lobster tank. *11.30am-11pm Mon-Sat*

A Casa da Rocha €€

33 A6

Arrive early for fresh fish and seats affording rock formation and Praia dos Três Castelos panoramas. *noon-10pm*

Vila Lisa €€€

34 A1

For fifty years, this drive-worthy, fixed-menu, homely restaurant has been serving typical and perfectly prepared Algarvian recipes. *hours vary*

Drinking

Carvoeiro Wine & Cocktails

Decadente Lounge

35 E3

Snug in a courtyard, this cosy wine bar is a great spot for an afternoon drink away from the sun while flame heaters warm winter nights. *11am-9pm Mon-Sat*

Sky Bar Carvoeiro

36 F4

Facing secluded Praia de Vale Covo, the Tivoli Hotel's rooftop bar is a serene sunset spot (not to be confused with the sky bar at Carvoeiro beach, though it's also excellent) *6-10pm*

Rolha Wine Bar

37 H2

In Porches, expect a warm welcome, personalised Portuguese grape recommendations, *petiscos* (small plates) and chit-chat with the sociable owner. *6-11.30pm Thu-Sun*

Ferragudo Live Music

Club Nau

38 C6

Enjoy front-row views of Praia Grande from the fusion bar-restaurant or beach bucket chairs with sunset DJs, bands, and an excellent cocktail menu. *10am-10pm*

Os Três Macacos

39 C5

With a chatty team and a quaint enclosed courtyard, this is a cracking bar any day of the week, though Friday's live music sessions pull in the crowds. *9pm-2am Mon-Sat*

Praia da Rocha & Alvor Bars

Outro Bar

40 A6

Praia da Rocha has plenty of cliff-topping bars that go into the early hours; come here on Sunday afternoons for live music. *3pm-4am*

Michael's Bar

41 A2

After a long stint at Carvoeiro's Jailhouse (sadly now closed), the couple-run bar reopened in Alvor, bringing their nightly live music with them. *6pm-2am Mon-Sat*

Caniço

42 B3

Step into a cliff-built lift and descend to this secluded bay for beach drinks or summer parties; skip the disappointing restaurant. *9.30am-2am*

Shopping

Markets

convent'bio

43 G2

Lagoa's premier organic produce store, which grows vegetables on-site and bakes bread, is a great place to stock up. There's also a small cafe inside the former convent. *9am-6pm Mon-Fri*

Mercado Municipal de Portimão

44 A4

Large, clean, central market in Portimão with a butcher, fresh fish, bakery and plenty of farm-fresh produce. *7am-2pm Mon-Sat*

Beauty

Aloegarve

see 35

Stock up on organic aloe vera products produced in the Algarve at this local chain's Carvoeiro branch. *10am-6pm*

See p127 for eating and drinking listings

Explore Silves & Monchique

Scented by citrus and almond blossoms, soundtracked by birdsong, flanked by fantastic wineries, and fronted by the Rio Arade, inland Silves is bucolic and timeless. The chronology of the final capital of Al-Gharb – Xilb, as it was called during Moorish rule – and later, the Algarve Kingdom, is recounted across Islamic poet murals, Moorish museums, and inside the hulking sandstone castle's walls, while modern life, markets and ceramic studios shape the inviting labyrinth of streets below. Beyond, the Serra de Monchique mountain range climbs to Fóia, the Algarve's highest peak, with waterfall trails, artisans and Roman-loved sulphur-scented spas folded amongst its forests.

Getting Around

Walking

Silves' mainly pedestrianised, sometimes steep, centre and Monchique town are best explored on foot.

Car

Hire a car to explore the mountains freely. Taxis, handy for wineries, are in lesser supply.

Bus

From Silves to Monchique, use Vamus buses connecting in Portimão. Limited weekday services link Monchique with Marmelete and Alferce. Silves train station is a 2km walk away, including a short main road stretch.

Boat

Arriving along the Rio Arade is dreamy; boat tours depart from Portimão (p109).

THE BEST

HISTORIC SITE Castelo de Silves (p124)

WINERY TOUR Quinta de Mata Mouros (p120)

HIKING VIEWPOINT Fóia (p118)

EVENT Feira Medieval (p126)

ACTIVITY Sweet Making Workshops (p124)

Silves

A
B
C
D
1
2
3
4
5
6
Ribeira da Cerca
Marmelete
10
Casa do Medronho
Pico da Fóia
18
Monchique
20
21
Quadsexperience
Parque Fonte dos Amores
Caldas de Monchique
Ribeira de Odiáxere
Ribeira da Torre
Ribeira de Boina
Autódromo Internacional do Algarve
11
Ribeira do Farelo
Barragem dos Álamos
Castelo Belinho
Barragem do Morgado
For more see
Top Experiences p118
Experiences p124
Eating p127
Drinking p127
Via do Infante
0 4 km
0 2 miles

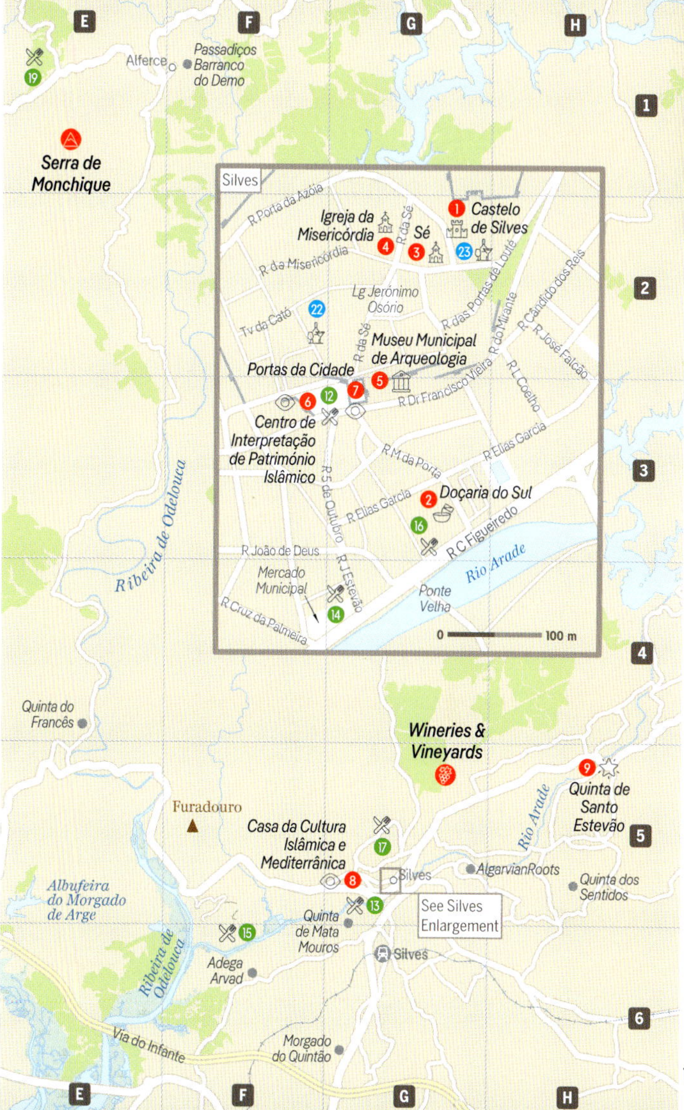
Alferce
Passadiços Barranco do Demo
Serra de Monchique
Silves
R Porta da Azóia
Igreja da Misericórdia
R da Sé
Sé
Castelo de Silves
R da Misericórdia
Lg Jerónimo Osório
Tv da Cató
R das Portas de Loulé
R do Mirante
R Cândido dos Reis
R José Falcão
R da Sé
Museu Municipal de Arqueologia
Portas da Cidade
R Dr Francisco Vieira
R L Coelho
Centro de Interpretação de Património Islâmico
R M da Porta
R Elias Garcia
R 5 de Outubro
R Elias Garcia
Doçaria do Sul
R C Figueiredo
R João de Deus
Mercado Municipal
R J Estevão
Rio Arade
Ponte Velha
R Cruz da Palmeira
0
100 m
Ribeira de Odelouca
Quinta do Francês
Wineries & Vineyards
Quinta de Santo Estevão
Rio Arade
Furadouro
Casa da Cultura Islâmica e Mediterrânica
Silves
AlgarvianRoots
Quinta dos Sentidos
See Silves Enlargement
Albufeira do Morgado de Arge
Quinta de Mata Mouros
Ribeira de Odelouca
Adega Arvad
Silves
Via do Infante
Morgado do Quintão

★ TOP EXPERIENCE

Serra de Monchique

Portugal's southwesternmost mountain range, the Serra de Monchique, is a land of native oaks, ancient laurels and elusive Bonelli's eagles best explored on foot. With more challenging treks around Fóia, the Algarve's highest peak, and easy-going ambles in Alferce, the car-accessible range has routes for all.

MAP P116 **E1**

PLANNING TIPS
The serra is prone to wildfires in summer; check for reports and warnings at *ipma.pt*. Mobile data can be unreliable in the mountains; download maps in advance.

Scan this QR code for detailed trail descriptions and to download GPX maps.

Hiking Trails

From 902m **Fóia**, the Algarve's highest point, the serra spills outwards, the ocean glistens beyond, and rugged trails begin. The 6.8km, circular Trilho da Fóia – one of around a dozen marked routes – is a well-rounded introduction to the area's endemic flora and livestock; tack on the moderate 10km forested extension to reach the Cascata do Barbelote waterfall. It's possible to trek between Silves and Monchique on the most challenging 32km stretch (sector 10) of the Algarve-crossing **Via Algarviana** (p82), passing through streams, abandoned villages and thermal springs.

A Serene Suspension Bridge

Completed at the end of 2023, the 1km **Passadiços Barranco do Demo** in Alferce is an easy-going, staired wooden walkway with a valley-crossing suspension bridge. For a longer stroll, a 7.8km extension crosses the valley's river on foot. The car park behind the cemetery fills up quickly; consider walking from the hamlet.

Thermal Springs

Revered since Roman times, the Serra de Monchique's thermal waters are renowned for their restorative high alkaline (9.5pH) levels. The main cluster is in **Caldas de Monchique**, a whimsical mountain village 10 minutes south of Monchique.

Suspension bridge, Alferce
SOPOTNICKI/SHUTTERSTOCK ©

Termas de Monchique Spa Resort (*monchiquetermalresort.com; prices vary*) offers treatments and spa circuits for non-staying guests. For a more natural experience, follow the **Parque Fonte dos Amores**' short, uphill trail tracking trickling streams for a shaded picnic and to spot locals filling up supermarket-sold branded bottles from the source. From here, a challenging, 18km circular trail climbs to 774m Picota.

Mountain Tours

Various companies operate guided hikes, including Silves-departing **AlgarvianRoots** (*algarvianroots.com; prices vary*); their most interesting excursion combines trails with olive oil mill visits or pottery workshops. **Quadsexperience** (*quadsexperience.com; from €125*) offers half-day quad bike tours.

QUICK BREAK
Stop by locally loved **Café Império** (*12.30-3pm & 7-9pm Thu-Mon*) near Caldas de Monchique for a fair-priced chicken piri-piri feast. Snag a back terrace table for verdant valley views.

★ TOP EXPERIENCE

Wineries & Vineyards

Vines were first planted around Silves by the Phoenicians. Over the last decade, a new wave of vintners has revitalised the scene. Now, contemporary wineries, creative blends and late-night events complement ancient amphorae ageing methods, making Silves an excellent spot for a tour and tasting.

MAP P116 **G5**

PLANNING TIPS
Most wineries only open on weekdays and require advance bookings for tours. Confirm directions when booking; GPS directions often miss the correct entrance to larger vineyards.

Scan this QR code for more on wine tourism experiences available across the Algarve.

The Algarve's Wines

The Algarve wine region is divided into four Controlled Denominations of Origin (DOC): Lagos, Portimão, Tavira, and the largest, Lagoa – though the boundaries don't respect their namesake cities. Silves falls within Lagoa's DOC, and thanks to its scenery, mineral-rich sloped terrain and multiple international investments, it has become one of the Algarve's best wine destinations. Typical grapes include indigenous Negra Mole and Crato Branco; Touriga Nacional, considered Portugal's finest, is also prevalent. While red wines were long favoured, whites and interesting rosés are now well represented.

Tours & Tastings

Silves' nearest and arguably most impressive winery is the historic forested estate of **Quinta de Mata Mouros** (*conventodoparaiso.com; from €20*). Alongside tastings, estate manager Laura conducts vine tours in a 1980s Land Rover, visiting the 15th-century convent linked to legends of Moorish tunnels. At contemporary **Quinta dos Sentidos** (*qds.pt; from €30*), private tours by the owners or winemaker André take in the experimental vineyard and well-manicured fruit gardens and vines before tasting forward-thinking wines and olive oil. Rustic-feeling **Quinta do Francês** (*quintadofrances.com; from €13.50*) doesn't require a reservation for

DANIEL JAMES CLARKE ©

tastings on the sunny, vineyard-viewing terraces, but you'll need to book for a quick but informative tour.

Special Events & Experiences

For a memorable meal served under the shade of a 2000-year-old olive tree, reserve a space for the weekday, wine-paired communal lunches at **Morgado do Quintão** (*morgadodoquintao.pt; from €42.50*), an expansive estate founded by the Count of Silves in the early 1800s. Equally as unforgettable is arriving at **Adega Arvad** (*arvad.pt; tastings from €30*) on a Rio Arade boat trip from Portimão (*algarvesunboat.com; €68*) to sip 100% Negra Mole produced in Phoenician-style amphorae. The winery also offers picnics and sunset sessions. It's always worth asking vineyards about upcoming events, as fado performances and banquet dinners are often scheduled. Silves council organises multi-winery **Jazz nas Adegas** (*cm-silves.pt*) concerts in winter and spring.

JOIN A HARVEST

Wine harvest experiences are the calendar highlight, especially those traditionally treading grapes. While usually in September, drought and the changing climate mean some recent harvests have commenced in August.

Drive Silves & Monchique

Forgo hiking boots and savour Silves' citrus-coated scenery and the Serra de Monchique's easy-access viewpoints on this full-day driving tour. En route, sample local flavours and meet the makers producing wine, olive oil, ceramics and woodcrafts. Weekdays work best to ensure attractions are open.

START	END	LENGTH
Silves	Caldas de Monchique	79km; 1¾ hours

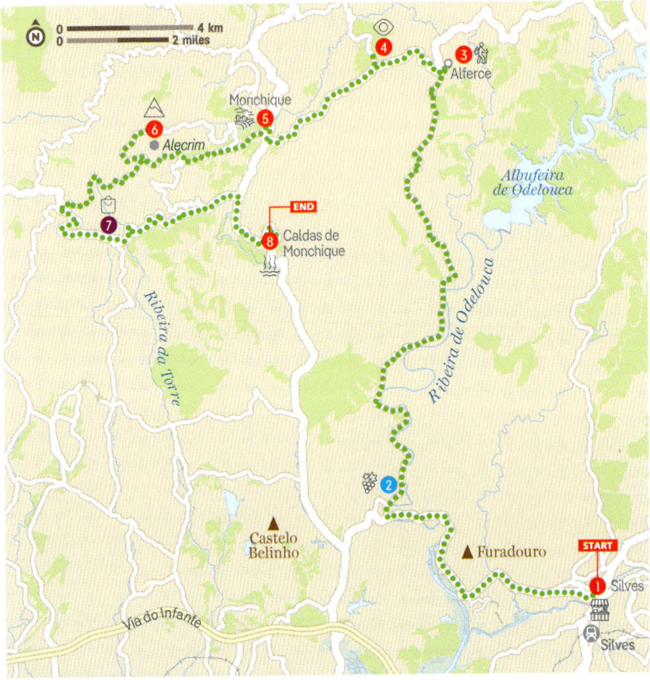

1 Local Flavours

Swing by Silves' **Mercado Municipal** (*7am to 2pm Monday to Saturday*) to stock up on the city's signature citrus fruits or enjoy a sit-down breakfast at the suitably named **Divine Sweetness** next door.

2 Wine & Dine

Drive to **Quinta do Francês** winery, where the vineyard-view tasting terrace opens at 10am. Alternatively, prebook the 11.30am one-hour tour and tasting, followed by lunch at nearby **Casa De Pasto A Parreirinha**. The typical rural restaurant has fair-priced corkage, so non-designated drivers can bring a bottle.

3 Suspension Bridge Stretch

Meander inland on rural roads, slicing through citrus groves into the mountains. Stretch your legs at the teeny village of **Alferce** on the 1km **Passadiços Barranco do Demo** boardwalk and suspension bridge.

4 Liquid Gold

Driving west, detour to **Lagar dos Pardieiros** (*azeitemonchique.com; from €32*), an old-fashioned, family-run olive oil mill, for a private, prebooked tour and sampling of the mountain's liquid gold.

5 Ceramics & Strolls

Park up in woodland-cocooned **Monchique** for an amble. The 15th-century **Igreja Matriz** is the main architectural site with its five-starred Manueline doorway. Find some excellent artisans here, including **Studio Bongard**'s ceramic workshop, which displays colourful and creative pieces across a characterful garden, and Atelier da Clara's private pottery classes. **Republica Clandesitina** distils gin and produces fiery, chilli-infused condiments. Just west, the once impressive convent is now overgrown, neglected, dangerous and usually occupied by squatters.

6 The Algarve's Highest Peak

There's no need to hike to 902m **Fóia**; you'll find a car park and miradouro (lookout) right at the top. Take in the sweeping forest and ocean views from a deckchair at the food truck **Alecrim** just below.

7 Repurposed Wood

Continuing west, **WoodSpirit Gallery** displays José's countless artistic carvings, crafted from collected native Algarve and Portuguese woods. The gallery is deceptively large, and the shop sells larger and smaller pieces from €15. Hours are erratic, depending on when José is at home.

8 Thermal Waters

End with a wander through **Caldas de Monchique**, where easy-going uphill steps track the thermal springs.

EXPERIENCES

Explore the Magnificent Moorish Castle

CASTLE

MAP: 1 P116 **G2**

The impressive and well-renovated **Castelo de Silves** (*cm-silves.pt; €2.10/including museum €3.90*) is the Algarve's crowning castle. Constructed in the 10th century over a likely Roman fortress, it was from here that the Moors and, later, the first Christian Kings ruled the region. Circle the ramparts and peer through the crenellated russet sandstone walls to survey the citrus-scented scene, overlooking the carob and almond trees introduced by the Moors. According to legend, King Ibn-Almundim planted the latter for his beloved snow-missing Princess Gilda, who hailed from the Nordics. After walking through the ruined Almohad dwelling walls inside the castle, the occasional sign and modern embellishment showing how the internal village might have once looked descend into the now dry cisterns. Information on the nearby, not-visitable Iberian Lynx conservation and re-introduction centre is displayed in the underground space. There are some ramps inside the castle, but no lifts for the walls and cisterns. Concerts are scheduled inside the castle over the summer.

Make Silves' Signature Sweet Treats

WORKSHOP

MAP: 2 P116 **G3**

No excuse is needed to visit **Doçaria do Sul** (*docariadosul.pt; prices vary*), an adorable cafe and shop serving all local flavours, including carob coffee, the freshest orange juice, and almond, fig and orange sweet treats. Yet there is another, tastier reason: Silvina and her team host traditional, handmade sweet workshops. Over two-hour sessions, you'll be taught to prepare typical *doce fino* or *torta de laranja* (an orange roll), depending on the season. The classes are low-key, chatty and use all local ingredients, ending with a box of your creations to take away.

REGIONAL CAKES & SWEETS

Lisbon's *pastel de nata* (custard tart) is Portugal's most fabled sweet, but the Algarve's regional fig, carob and almond cakes shouldn't be skipped. The most prevalent are *doce fino*, small, colourful marzipan delicacies shaped like fruits or animals; the sticky, sweet egg-and-cinnamon *Dom Rodrigos*, wrapped up like shiny gifts; and dome-shaped, white-fondant-coated *morgadinhos*, filled with eggy almond paste. Silves' circular *queijo de figos* are baked with figs, almonds and brandy, and the honey and almond *torta de alfarroba* replaces chocolate with carob flour. In summer, beach vendors sell *bolas de Berlim* – custard-stuffed, no-hole doughnuts.

Reflect on the Religious Reconquista

CHURCH

Following the Reconquista, Xilb's mosque was replaced with a Gothic cathedral, **Sé** (MAP: 3 P116 **G2**; *cm-silves.pt; €2*). Earthquake-damaged and regularly reconstructed, much of today's structure is from the 18th century, which explains why, once inside, it feels less impressive than the hulking exterior presents. Still, it's worth a brief visit (wear suitable clothes; shawls otherwise provided) to see the soaring sandstone columns. Just don't expect an overly elaborate altar or side chapels. The **Igreja da Misericórdia** (MAP: 4 P116 **G2**) opposite occasionally hosts free art exhibitions.

Admire Moorish Artefacts & Archaeology

MUSEUM

MAP: 5 P116 **G3**

Anchored around an excavated, 18m-deep Almohad cistern-well, descendible in part via a narrow internal staircase, the **Museu Municipal de Arqueologia** (*cm-silves.pt; €2.10*) is a Moorish time capsule. Closed on Mondays, the three-storey space displays the town's history, from prehistoric tombstones to Roman coins. But Silves' Muslim period takes the spotlight, with collections covering the Umayyad, Caliphate, Taifa, Almoravid and Almohad periods. You can access and walk atop a section of the old walls from the top floor.

Take a Deeper Moorish Dive

TRAILS/TOURS

If you're keen to follow the Algarve's Moorish trail further, visit the weekday-only **Centro de Interpretação de Património Islâmico** (MAP: 6 P116 **F3**) on the square facing **Portas da Cidade** (MAP: 7 P116 **G3**), the sole surviving upper door and tower. Brief Moorish history is shared inside, and the team can provide detailed maps for two region-crossing, Moorish-tracing itineraries, the **Umayyad Route** and the **Al-Mutamid Route**, alongside arranging tours to Silves' **Casa da Cultura Islâmica e Mediterrânica** (MAP: 8 P116 **G5**; *cm-silves.pt; hours vary*), a neo-Mudejar building dedicated to Arabic words and culture in Portugal.

Visit a Family-Run Orange Farm

FARM

MAP: 9 P116 **H5**

The Moors planted the first oranges in Silves – the bitter type that led to the Portuguese word for quince paste, *marmelo*, preceding what the British call marmalade – but the Age of Discovery brought sweet oranges from Asia. Now, four varieties of orange grow from November until August, plus clementines in autumn, giving Silves a year-round supply. For a farm-fresh experience, book a visit to **Quinta de Santo Estevão** (*quinta-santo-estevao.pt; from €15*), a centuries-old working

MEET MARMELETE'S MEDRONHO MAKERS

In Marmelete, an easily-overlooked village 20 minutes west of Monchique, the red strawberry-like fruits of the *medronho* tree are the prized local produce. For centuries, locals have distilled the berries to create strong and fiery *aguardente* (firewater). Learn more at the small, weekday-only **Casa do Medronho** (*casadomedronho.com; €1.50*), which explains the fruit-to-firewater process; you'll occasionally find the fire burning and the process in full swing. It's possible to join some local distillers to pick fruit and partake in the home-brewing. Email or call well ahead to make arrangements for this more personal experience.

MAP: 10 P116 **A2**

farm with donkeys, horse riding, and extensive citrus groves where José leads 90-minute farm tours and picking sessions. The Rota da Laranja App (*visitalgarve.pt*) highlights other citrus-focused trails and experiences.

Step Back in Time During the Medieval Festival

FESTIVAL

For around ten days every August, Silves steps back in time for the annual **Feira Medieval** (*feiramedievaldesilves.pt*). From humble beginnings in 1996, today it's an all-encompassing explosion of sounds, sights and flavours. Every year has a different theme, but historical reenactments – both from Islamic and Christian periods – costumed performers, veiled flame-juggling dancers, music, jousting tournaments and 'Berber tents' hawking traditional wares are all constants. Children are entertained at the evening Xilb dos Pequenos' pottery and *azulejos* (hand-painted tiles) workshops. Year-round, Silves and Monchique host numerous smaller festivals and events, often focusing on local food specialities, such as *chouriças* (pork sausages), and folklore traditions – find agendas on municipal websites: *cm-silves.pt and cm-monchique.pt.*

Drive on a One-Time F1 Track

SUPERCARS

MAP: 11 P116 **B4**

Get your speed kicks in a supercar at the **Autódromo Internacional do Algarve** (*autodromodoalgarve.com; from €195*), where the only-ever Portuguese Grand Prix was hosted in 2021. There are a few different experiences to book, though the chance to drive some laps in a revved-up supercar (under professional supervision) is the most exhilarating. There's also a go-kart track for more family-friendly fun.

LISTINGS

Best Places for...

See p116 for map of locations

€ Budget €€ Midrange €€€ Top End

Eating

Silves Cafes

DaRosa €
12 G3
This cafe's interior is as pretty as its shaded-terrace views of the square's fountain. *9am-5pm Mon-Fri, 10am-3pm Sat*

Chapim €
13 G5
On the grassy riverbank, this easy-going cafe serves drinks and snacks, and is fantastic for families thanks to the playground next door. *9am-7pm*

Silves Restaurants

Churrasqueira Valdemar €
14 G4
This Silves Market terrace fills fast at lunch as workers arrive for mixed grills and chicken piri-piri. *noon-3pm & 6.30-10pm Mon-Sat*

Clube Nautico €
15 F6
It's a dirt-track drive to this cheerful riverside BBQ and bar with upstream Silves views and a summer pool. *noon-5pm Fri-Mon*

Nova Mesquita €

16 G3
Traditional, home-style cooking makes this a reliable everyday option, though it's best booked on Thursday nights for fado performances. *noon-3pm & 6-10pm Mon-Sat*

Recanto Dos Mouros €€
17 G5
This glorious restaurant with castle views deserves a reservation (or two) for its traditional dishes, including *javali* (wild boar) and lamb stew. *noon-2.30pm & 7-10pm Thu-Tue.*

Monchique Meals

Alecrim €

18 C1
After reaching Fóia's viewpoint, descend a little to this food truck for a well-deserved burger and beer while resting in a deckchair. *1-8pm*

Restaurante Malhada Quente €

19 E1
Get your freshly grilled chicken piri-piri fix at this roadside stop. *11.30am-3pm & 6.30-9:30pm Tue-Sun*

O Parque €

20 D1
Central, wholesome restaurant grilling typical and hearty mountain meat dishes such as boar, black pork, lamb and daily specials. *9am-11pm Fri-Wed*

Jardim das Oliveiras €€
21 D1
Bucolic setting with shaded gardens and a wooden-beamed dining room (and winter fireplace) serving meat-heavy specialities. *noon-3.30pm & 6.30pm-9.30pm Wed-Mon*

Drinking

Silves Bars

Segredo dos Mouros

22 F2
Easily missed, this quaint cafe and wine bar has a 'no smoking' balcony overlooking the ochre rooftops. *11am-5pm Thu-Mon*

Café Inglês

23 G2
Popular bar-restaurant on the wide stairs leading to the castle with local brews, wines, sangria and Sunday afternoon music sessions. *10am-11.30pm Tue-Sun*

See p140
for eating,
drinking and
shopping
listings

Explore Lagos

With craggy coves, sweeping sands, and the ragged, spotlight-stealing Ponta da Piedade headland on its doorstep, Lagos' partly-walled Old Town is a cracking coastal city base. Yet, for all its laid-back charm, the city played an oversized historical role. Portugal's first Age of Discovery caravels set sail from here, leading affluent Lagos to be crowned regional capital in 1576, a title it lost after the 1755 tsunami tore through. Nowadays, Lagos is much more subdued, with sunrise yoga sessions, street art, leisurely seafood lunches, and dolphin-spotting boat trips on the menu. That is, until after dark, when eclectic nightlife abounds.

Getting Around

Walking

Lagos' compact, mainly pedestrianised centre, easy-access beaches, scenic board-walks and trails to Ponta da Piedade and Luz make it a fantastic car-free base.

Bus

The city's Onda buses, with accessibility ramps, serve Meia Praia, Luz, and the nearby interior; pay onboard. The intercity bus station is adjacent to the Old Town; beach buses depart from near the market. Lagos' is the westernmost rail terminus.

Kayak

Opt for kayaking over boat tours to access tucked-away sands and fully appreciate the coastline.

THE BEST

KAYAK ADVENTURE Ponta da Piedade (p132)

MUSEUM Museu de Lagos (p136)

VINEYARD Monte da Casteleja (p138)

HIKE Fisherman's Trail to Luz (p138)

FADO Café Vádio (p140)

Praia do Camilo **(p136)**

A
B
C
D
1
2
3
4
5
6
7
Via do Infante
Lagos
Mercado Municipal
15
Centro Ciência Viva de Lagos
5
Lagos Marina
8
R Dr Faria e Silva
Pç Gil Eanes
23
Rio Bensafrim
R Gil Eanes
R Garret
Pç Luís de Camões
Lg Marquês de Pombal
R da Barroca
Av dos Descobrimentos
28
22
R I de Maio
R da Oliveira
R Marreiros Neto
R da Extrema
R 25 de Abril
R Dr Joaquim Tello
R do Ferrador
20
Mercado de Escravos
11
Pç Infante Dom Henrique
R Cândido dos Reis
R da Silva Lopes
R Prof Luís Azevedo
31
32
Igreja de Santo António
10
Centro Cultural
18
R Gil Vicente
0
100 m
Museu de Lagos
9
Estrada do Paúl
Monte da Casteleja Vineyard
12
Aeródromo de Lagos
Av da Fonte Coberta
26
Av Paul Harris
Av Christóvão Colombo
Estrada da Atalaia
R 1º de Maio
R Direita
Luz
14
Praia da Luz
27
13
Vinha da Falésia
4
Praia de Porto de Mós
ATLANTIC OCEAN
A
B
C
D

E F G H

1 2 3 4 5 6

Estrada da Meia Praia

Rio Alvor

16 OstraSelect

17 Algarve Balloons

Meia Praia

21

Estrada da Meia Praia

Tourist Train

6

Lagos

LAC

19 30

Doca Pesca

25

1 Meia Praia

See Lagos Enlargement

Lagos

ATLANTIC OCEAN

Kayak Explorers

29

3 Praia dos Estudantes

Passadiços da Ponta da Piedade

24

Praia do Camilo 2

Estrada da Ponta da Piedade

Ponta da Piedade

For more see

Top Experiences p132
Experiences p136
Eating p140
Drinking p140
Shopping p141

0 2 km
0 1 mile

★ TOP EXPERIENCE

Ponta da Piedade

Lagos' ocean-sculpted headland and cinematic coastline begs to be explored, and countless boat tour operators ply the waters around Ponta da Piedade. However, the sandstone cliffs, sea stacks, and striking panoramas can also be relished from the cliff-topping boardwalk, or kayak for a close-up experience.

MAP P130 **E6**

PLANNING TIPS
Sunsets are spectacular but busy; plan a sunrise visit for serenity. Buses don't run to the headland; the tourist train does. The nearest (free) parking is 700m from the lighthouse.

Scan this QR code for a list of boat trip operators based at Lagos Marina.

On Foot

Reaching the lighthouse-crowned headland on foot became easier in 2024 with the completion of the 2km **Passadiços da Ponta da Piedade**, a wooden boardwalk constructed to ease erosion and protect the landscape. The first section of the path begins above Praia do Pinhão (turn down R. José Formosinho); the beach itself closed due to a cliff collapse in 2024. At Praia da Dona Ana, cross the car park to rejoin the boardwalk via stairs near the roundabout. A step-free, more accessible section begins near **Praia do Camilo**'s (p136) gravel car park. From here, the path has a handful of detours to unshaded ocean-viewing platforms along the final stretch. Just beyond the non-public lighthouse (and a coin-operated WC), Ponta da Piedade's stone-carved stairs are the dramatic finale, descending to a water-splashed boat landing cocooned by rock formations. The boardwalk continues west of the headland towards Praia do Canavial, followed by the cliff-top trail to **Luz** (p139).

Kayak Tours

The best views of the Costa d'Oiro (Golden Coast) are arguably from the water. **Kayak Explorers**' (*lagoskayakexplores.com; €35*) two- to three-hour

D.BOND/SHUTTERSTOCK ©

town-departing tours include otherwise inaccessible caves and a shoreline snorkelling stop. Book the earliest trip to avoid congestion around the grottos. If renting equipment, be aware that new regulations (punishable by fine) were introduced in 2024 to restrict boards and similar from being carried on the staircases of Praia da Dona Ana and Praia do Camilo between 9am-7pm, June to September.

Boat Trips

While multiple tours depart from the marina, combining the boardwalk with a boat trip will maximise your experience. **Grotto Pioneers** (*instagram.com/grottopioneers; from €20 cash*), boarding from Ponta da Piedade's staircase base, have been running tours for a century, using small fishing boats to reach hidden spots.

SNACK BREAK
Daytime-only **Sol Nascente** is nearest, serving ice creams, drinks, and light meals. **O Camilo** has ocean views; Praia do Porto de Mos has several beachside restaurants.

Walk Lagos' Old Town

Discover Lagos' contemporary creativity and age-old maritime links on this Old Town amble, blending street art, seafaring stories and pretty squares. From the modern marina to a former fort, the walk crosses museums and attractions before easily feeding into the Passadiços da Ponta da Piedade boardwalk.

START	END	LENGTH
Boa Esperança Caravel Ship	Forte da Ponta da Bandeira	2.8km; 1 hour

1 Marina Memories

Start at the replica **Boa Esperança Caravel**, which houses a compact Age of Discovery interpretation centre (*prebook access: 282 770 000*), before crossing the bridge linking the modern **marina** with palm-lined **Avenida dos Descobrimentos**.

2 Street Art & Science

Follow the wide promenade, often lined with mass-produced market stalls, before crossing to **Rua da Marombeira**'s steps, decorated with an annually changing collection of street art posters. Circle around **Igreja de São Sebastião** to reach the art-adorned **Centro Ciência Viva de Lagos**.

3 Seafood Stalls

Stairs outside the museum descend into the **Mercado Municipal** (*8am to 2pm Monday to Saturday*), with fresh produce and even fresher caught seafood. Exit the market on the ground floor towards the pedestrianised Old Town.

4 Pretty Squares

Cross the two pretty squares of **Praça Gil Eanes** and especially photogenic **Praça Luís de Camões** – named after Luís Vaz de Camões, author of Os Lusíadas, an epic poem celebrating Portugal's ocean exploration – to **Rua Infante de Sagres**, carpeted with striking *calçadas portuguesas* (Portuguese cobblestone pavements).

5 Muralhas & Murals

Reaching the remaining Moorish-built, later reinforced *muralhas* (walls), return downtown towards the **Centro Cultural** for more colourful murals; the most impressive is the blue-and-white *azulejo*-inspired piece by artist Fuel. The **Museu de Lagos** and Igreja de Santo António are nearby.

6 Horrific History

Reflect at the history-defining **Praça do Infante Dom Henrique**, the location of the **Mercado de Escravos**, Europe's first slave market. A statue of Prince Henry the Navigator (Dom Henrique), the catalyst for Portugal's empire-expanding Age of Discovery, stands in the middle. Peek in dimly lit **Igreja de Santa Maria** and the 17th-century **Armazém Regimental**, a former shipping storehouse turned teeny art gallery.

7 A Grand Gateway

Follow the sturdy walls of the 17th-century **Castelo dos Governadores** to the twin-tower-flanked **Arco de São Gonçalo**. Inside the thick archway, there's a small shrine in the reported birthplace of Lagos' patron saint of fishermen, São Gonçalo.

8 Fort Finale

Finish by crossing 17th-century **Forte da Ponta da Bandeira**'s drawbridge to relish ocean views from the ramparts.

EXPERIENCES

Pick Your Perfect Shoreline

BEACH ACTIVITES

Lagos' beaches are as much about water sports as sunbathing. Sweeping and accessible (amphibious wheelchair available), **Meia Praia** (MAP: 1 P130 F4) is a popular kitesurfing spot, with numerous schools offering lessons and rentals. Classes can also be taken at the estuary or inland wakeboard park. Gorgeous, pocket-sized **Praia do Camilo** (MAP: 2 P130 E5) is the place to get your steps in via the 200-plus stepped staircase descending to the cliff-hugged cove. If you'd prefer to paddle at your own pace, hire a SUP board and splash around **Praia dos Estudantes**' Roman-style bridge spanning two rocks (MAP: 3 P130 E4). Surfers will find the nearest reef break at **Praia de Porto de Mós** (MAP: 4 P130 D5).

Spot Dolphins in the Wild

BOAT TRIPS

MAP: 8 P130 C1

Boat trips of all kinds depart from Lagos' modern marina. Most head to Ponta da Piedade (p132), while some turn east towards Benagil Cave (p104). One of the best dolphin-watching operators is **SeaLife** (*sealife.pt; adult/child €40/€25*). A marine biologist is onboard every trip, which ensures an environmental focus and helps their tours to achieve a reported 96% sighting rate. If you'd prefer to explore underwater, **WeDive** (*wedive.pt*) offers scuba courses for all levels and guided shipwreck dives.

See a Dazzling Church & Collection

MUSEUM/CHURCH

The city's main museum, **Museu de Lagos** (MAP: 9 P130 C4; *museu.*

THE 1755 EARTHQUAKE

On 1 November 1755, life across Portugal changed forever as an 8.7 magnitude quake, and a subsequent tsunami, left a trail of death and destruction. Referred to as the Lisbon Earthquake, due to the capital suffering severe damage, the epicentre was actually 200km southwest of the Algarve's **Cabo de São Vicente** (p148). Much of coastal Algarve was decimated, especially Lagos, which lost its regional capital crown. For this reason, most regional architecture is at least partially reconstructed.

cm-lagos.pt; adult/child €3/€1.50), closed Mondays, also affords access to the astonishing **Igreja de Santo António** (MAP: 10 P130 **C4**). With a sometimes mismatched collection, mainly donated by amateur archaeologist Dr José Formosinho, each of the museum's rooms covers a separate period. Ornate *azulejos* (hand-painted tiles), religious canvases and triptychs, and Algarvian history, including costumes, crafts and typical home recreations, are all visitable within an hour. Ending with the showstopper, the 18th-century church is awash with blue-and-white *azulejos*, crowned with a trompe-l'oeil ceiling, and dazzles with baroque gilding, depicting Roman soldiers and Moorish characters. The museum has tactile flooring and some braille panels.

BEST ACTIVITIES WITH KIDS

Centro Ciência Viva de Lagos

MAP: 5 P130 **B1**

Lagos' engaging science museum, closed Mondays, is dedicated to ocean exploration, with interactive elements including a miniature visitable lighthouse (*lagos.cienciaviva.pt; adult/child €6/€3*).

Tourist Train

MAP: 6 P130 **E3**

Take it easy on this city-touring train on wheels with single tickets to Ponta da Piedade and city-wide hop-on-hop-off passes (*touristtrainlagos.com; €5.50*).

Parque Zoológico de Lagos

MAP: 7 P130 **A1**

Lagos' out-of-town zoo has animal petting, penguins, monkeys and a swimming pool (*zoolagos.com; adult/child €15.83/€11.18 online*).

Reflect at Europe's First Slave Market

MUSEUM

MAP: 11 P130 **C3**

When a naval fleet set sail to conquer Ceuta in 1415, Lagos' story became forever entwined with the Age of Discovery. Over the following decades, caravels embarked on colonising missions and returned with enslaved Africans. **Mercado de Escravos** (*cm-lagos.pt; €3*), the likely location of Europe's first slave market, opened in 1444. The market, now a two-storey museum, acknowledges the lives of those enslaved via stories, facts, maps and digital displays. Still, in some areas, it lacks depth, delivering certain details from a colonialist viewpoint. In 2009, over 150 African skeletons were uncovered in Lagos' centuries-old landfill, investigated in the 2023 essay-like film *Tales of Oblivion* directed by Angolan-born Dulce Fernandes.

Parque Zoológico de Lagos (p137)

Sip Wine Amongst Vines

VINEYARDS

Lagos isn't lacking for wine bars, but if you prefer sipping biological wines with those that harvested them, cycle or take a 15-minute taxi to **Monte da Casteleja** (MAP: 12 P130 **D2**; *montecasteleja.com; from €25*). While production occurs offsite, walking through the vines – parts of the Roman city of Lacobriga buried beneath – and enjoying a relaxed Tuesday to Thursday afternoon two-hour tasting on the table is a pleasure. Prebook, and request their hard-to-find-elsewhere orange wine. Alternatively, venture to Portugal's southernmost vines atop the cliffs between Lagos and Luz at **Vinha da Falésia** (MAP: 13 P130 **C5**; *falesiawine.com; prices vary*). Planted in schist soil, the small-batch wines are mineral-rich. Samplings and tours in the wooden tasting room, with sweeping vine and ocean views, are bookable on request.

Hike the Cliffs to Luz

TRAIL

MAP: 14 P130 **A5**

The final 11km of the **Rota Vicentina Fisherman's Trail** (p146) links Lagos with the laid-back beach town of Luz, reducing to 6km if joined at Ponta da Piedade. Following a well-marked track, the reasonably easy route traverses atop Rocha Negra, a volcanic and sandstone cliff packed with fossils and Middle-Cretaceous-period traces. There's one short ascent at the end, but its more gradual when approached from Lagos. On arrival, take a dip at **Praia da Luz**, peer at the gated Roman ruins, and grab a snack at **Fortaleza da Luz** (p140), before returning to Lagos by bus.

Collect Fresh Oysters

SEAFOOD

Lagos' **Mercado Municipal** (MAP: 15 P130 B1) isn't short of freshly caught fish. Yet, even fresher oysters await at **OstraSelect** (MAP: 16 P130 H2; *+351 919 463 570*), a 25-minute drive from Lagos on the Meia Praia side of the Ria de Alvor Nature Reserve (p111). A working farm rather than an attraction, it's best to call or email to ensure Miguel or another team member is around for a low-tide visit. If so, they'll explain more about their Japanese Giga oysters while collecting you a surprisingly affordable bag. Wear wet-sand-suitable footwear.

Float Above it All

BALLOONING

MAP: 17 P130 E2

For a west coast aerial view, book a hot-air experience with **Algarve Balloons** (*algarveballoons.com; adult/child €195/€149*), based at Lagos' diminutive aerodrome. During summer, flights are only scheduled at sunset; sunrise take-offs are possible the rest of the year. While the wind dictates the final route around Lagos, the company also arrange flights around Portimão, Silves and Monchique.

BEST CULTURE & EVENTS

From street art exhibitions to contemporary theatre, there's always something creative boiling in Lagos - visit *cm-lagos.pt* for an updated events calendar.

Festa do Banho 29

Every 29 August, Lagos and especially Luz celebrate a bathing folklore legend with live music, a street party and midnight swims.

Centro Cultural

MAP: 18 P130 B4

Enjoy theatre, song, dance and activities year-round at the city's main cultural hub.

LAC

MAP: 19 P130 E4

Responsible for much of Lagos' street art, this 'creative laboratory' hosts contemporary exhibitions and workshops (*lac.org.pt*).

LISTINGS

Best Places for...

See p130 for map of locations

€ Budget €€ Midrange €€€ Top End

Eating

Brunch & Snacks

The Studio €
20 B3
Trendy cafe and photo gallery with in-house roasted coffee, home-made cakes, brunch dishes and co-working. There's a second branch in Luz. *7.30am-5.30pm*

Bar Quim €
21 G3
Shack-style spot at Meia Praia's peaceful far end for beers on the sand, or coffee and snacks on the terrace. *9am-6pm Mon-Sat*

Traditional Restaurants

Reis €€
22 A3
Long-standing, family-run restaurant serving reliable Algarvian dishes in a cosy dining room and on a teeny side-street terrace. *12.15-2.30pm & 6.15-10.30pm Mon-Sat*

Café Vádio €€

23 A2
One of Lagos' only places to watch fado. The ticketed performances on Tuesday and Friday evenings trump the included meal. *noon-midnight Mon-Sat*

Perfect Petiscos

Repolho Gastrobar €€
24 E5
Wine-stacked walls and small-plate recipes from across Portugal and its archipelagos; choose the 'surprise menu' with wine pairing for the full experience. *4-11pm Tue-Sun*

Tasca do Kiko €€
25 E4
Tucked behind the boatyard, the contemporary space has flavoursome sharing plates served with flair. *noon-3pm & 6-10pm Mon-Sat*

International Flavours

Cantinho de Minas €
26 D4
Enjoy a filling Brazilian feast at this unfussy restaurant, with quality *picanha* (rump steak) and, on Sundays, *feijoada* (black bean stew). *11am-11pm Wed-Mon*

Fortaleza da Luz €€

27 A5
Inside Luz's 17th-century fort, this landmark and ocean-view restaurant's menu has everything from burgers and steaks to ceviche and risotto. *11am-3pm & 6-9pm Wed-Mon*

Drinking

Cocktails & Craft Beers

Forbidden Door

28 A3
Ring the bell to enter this dimly lit and sophisti-

Igreja de São Sebastião (p135)

cated speakeasy where Welder and team mix uniquely Portuguese flavour-infused cocktails. *6pm-2am Thu-Tue*

The Collab

 E4

With local craft beers, like Lagos' Mania and Algoz's Marafada, organic wines and bao buns, the spacious terrace, sometimes soundtracked by live music, is sundowner perfection. *noon-11pm*

Shopping

Traditional Handicrafts

TEIAS

30 E4

Established by nine local artists, this contemporary and creative crafts shop sells cosmetics, art and ceramics. They also host monthly craft workshops. *11am-7pm Mon-Sat*

Mar d'Estórias

 B4

The ground floor of this restaurant sells a wide range of handmade and typically Portuguese gifts, making it one of Lagos' best souvenir shops. *10am-11pm*

Joalharia Santo Antonio

32 C4

Small boutique dedicated to fine gold and silver Portuguese filigree jewellery. *10am-6pm Mon-Fri*

See p156
for eating,
drinking and
shopping
listings

Explore Sagres & Costa Vicentina

Ocean-chiselled cliffs, footprint-free sands, dune-backed beaches and surf-pounded shores are only a fragment of the windswept west coast's magnetism. Juniper-scented, long-distance tracks ramble through perennial villages. Death-defying crustacean harvesters depart at daybreak. And Cabo de São Vicente, mainland Europe's most southwesterly corner, and the centuries-old hulking Fortaleza de Sagres, command respect. Stretching from Burgau to Odeceixe, where the Rio Seixe defines the regional border, the protected Parque Natural do Sudoeste Alentejano e Costa Vicentina is the Algarve's untamed coastal Eden.

Getting Around

Car

With remote beaches and rural detours, driving is recommended. Taxis and rideshares are limited; tour companies are an alternative. Off-roading and wild camping are prohibited.

Walking & Cycling

Ample cinematic trails make walking a joy. Some trails are bikeable; rent in Sagres.

Bus

Vamus 47 connects Sagres, Cabo de São Vicente, Salema, Burgau and Lagos. The weekday-only 79 runs between Odeceixe, Aljezur and Lagos; the 74 serves Aljezur and Arrifana; and the once-daily 22 links Vila do Bispo and Aljezur.

Praia da Bordeira (p153)

★

THE BEST

HISTORIC SITE Fortaleza de Sagres (p148)

COASTAL WALK Pontal da Carrapateira Trail (p153)

SURF CAMP Sagres Natura (p152)

BEACH Praia de Odeceixe (p153)

SEAFOOD A Sereia (p156)

Sagres
Praia da Beleceira
Porto da Baleeira
R Mestre
R do Mercado
R Dom Sebastião
R do Moreta
R Comandante Matoso
R P António Faustino
R de São Vicente
Mar Ilimitado
Sagres Natura Surf Camp
Praia da Mareta
ATLANTIC OCEAN
0 400 m
0 0.2 miles
Praia de Odeceixe
Praia das Adegas
Praia de Odeceixe
Odeceixe
Ribeira Seca
Rio Seixe
Rota Vicentina
Praia de Vale dos Homens
Rogil
Barranco da Galé
Praia da Amoreira
Burros & Artes
Área Protegida Privada Vale das Amoreiras
Museu Municipal
Ribeira da Cerca
Ribat da Atalaia
Castelo
Aljezur
Marmelete
Arrifana Surf School
Praia da Pedra da Agulha
Praia de Vale Figueira
Ribeira das Alfambras
Ribeira de Odiáxere
ATLANTIC OCEAN

Praia da Bordeira
Pontal da Carrapateira
Bordeira
Carrapateira
Museu do Mar e da Terra da Carrapateira
Povoado Islâmico de Pescadores
Albufeira de Odeáxere
Ribeira da Sobrosa
Via do Infante
Bensafrim
Mexilhoeira Grande
Odiáxere
Mata Nacional de Barão de São João
Barão de São João
Aldeia da Pedralva
Praia da Cordoama
Praia do Castelejo
Vila do Bispo Museum
Ribeira de Vale Barão
Barão de São Miguel
Lagos
Meia Praia
Lagos
Budens
Luz
Vila do Bispo
Coastline Algarve
Burgau
Salema
Parque Natural do Sudoeste Alentejano e Costa Vicentina
Menhir do Padrão
fossilised dinosaur footprints
Parque Natural do Sudoeste Alentejano e Costa Vicentina
South Kayaks
Cabo de São Vicente
Sagres
Divers Cape
Fortaleza de Sagres
See Sagres Enlargement
ATLANTIC OCEAN
For more see
Top Experiences p146
Experiences p152
Eating p156
Drinking p157
Shopping p157
0
10 km
0
5 miles
A
B
C
D
E
F
5
6
7
8

★ TOP EXPERIENCE

Rota Vicentina

The Costa Vicentina's primary draw for ramblers is the Rota Vicentina, two 13-day trails traversing the Algarve and Alentejo sections of the natural park. There's no need to pack an overnight bag – both break down into excellent one-day treks and are complemented by shorter circuits.

MAP P144 **D2**

PLANNING TIPS
Wildflower-decorated spring and autumn are the best times to hike. Routes are well signposted in either direction. Always carry enough water. Nature Treks (*naturetrekks.com*) provides luggage transfers for through-hikes.

Scan this QR code for trail maps, activities and guided tour companies.

Fisherman's Trail

The coast-hugging **Fisherman's Trail** (227km) has eight one-day Algarve sections between Odeceixe and Lagos, descending to footprint-free beaches and rising to thyme- and gorse-coated cliffs with endemic plants and birdlife. The final leg between **Luz and Lagos** (p138) is the easiest, intensity- and public-transport-wise. The moderate 17km Aljezur to Arrifana trail, via Praia de Monte Clérigo and Ribat da Atalaia's ruined Islamic fortress, also has weekday bus connections. The toughest stretch, the 19.5km trek between wild Sagres and slightly sheltered southern Salema, delivers diverse landscapes and Roman life remnants. From Odeceixe, a 12km, easy-going return walk crosses the Alentejo border to a swoon-worthy elevated viewpoint of horseshoe-shaped Praia de Odeceixe.

Historical Way

Slightly inland, the less-trafficked **Historical Way** (263km) concludes in Sagres, after five Algarvian sections crossing cork-coated, birdlife-teeming countryside and juniper-scented hinterlands with sporadic ocean views. Carrapateira to Vila do Bispo is a striking, leisurely and varied 21.4km walk (with an early morning 22 bus arrival), including a potential lunch stop at **Aldeia da Pedralva** (p155). For community-focused rambles, check for 'maintenance days' (*rotavicentina.com*) when volunteers join locals managing trail upkeep.

UMOMOS/SHUTTERSTOCK ©

Cycling

While most of the park's dedicated mountain-biking trails are further north around Alentejo's Odemira, some southern sections are bike-suited, including a two-day dedicated gravel bike route between Alentejo's Zambujeira do Mar and Cabo de São Vicente. Arrange support services and rentals online (*rotavicentina.com*). For shorter coastal scenes, cycle the **Pontal da Carrapateira Trail** (p153). Along the south coast, the 215km multi-day **Ecovia do Litoral** (part of EuroVelo1) connects Cabo de São Vicente with **Vila Real de Santo António** (p68) on rural trails, official bike paths (some markings are faded), and in parts, the main inland road.

Trail Markers

The Historical Way's signposting is red and white; the Fishermen's Trail's blue and green. There are four marker types: equals (follow), a cross (wrong way) and left and right arrows.

FROM THE ALENTEJO

Both 13-section trails begin in the Alentejo region near Sines (around 85km south of Lisbon; 2 hour Rede Expressos bus ride) at either São Torpes (Fishermen's) or Santiago do Cacém (Historical).

★ TOP EXPERIENCE

Fortaleza de Sagres & Cabo de São Vicente

Myths, legends, shipwrecks and sailors define Sagres and its end-of-the-world-feeling fortresses. Commandeering two separate, sheer headlands around 6km apart, a few hours spent here affords insights into Portugal's maritime might and the Age of Discovery; while windswept, low-key Sagres makes a great Costa Vicentina base.

MAP P144 **B8**

PLANNING TIPS
A scenic 7km coastal walk (watch out for gusts) and road-marked bike lane link the fortresses. Three bus connections run daily; afternoon schedules provide a better length of visit.

Scan this QR code for Fortaleza de Sagres' opening times.

Sagres' Fortress Promontory

Approaching the formidable, reconstructed, walkable ramparts of **Fortaleza de Sagres** (*promontoriode sagres.pt; €3*), one imagines a robust defence system beyond. In reality, it's a barren headland hosting some 15th-century structures that survived the 1755 earthquake. Thankfully, an Age of Discovery interactive exhibition opened in 2023, providing historical context via nautical charts and presentations covering the fortress, caravels and trade routes. Outside, there's a sealed 16th-century chapel, cistern tower, and a remarkable, overgrown, 43m-wide floor-level stone compass. Trails (some accessible) and information boards spread across the wide, weathered promontory towards cliff-perched fishers and the maze-like A Voz do Mar installation, echoing the roaring waves far below.

The 'Edge of Europe' Lighthouse

Crowning the ocean-ravaged **Cabo de São Vicente** headland, 16th-century **Fortaleza do Cabo de São Vicente** denotes mainland Europe's southwestern-most point. The interior of the originally 18th-century lighthouse only opens its small museum on summer Wednesday afternoons (at the time of research, it was closed indefinitely), but the main attraction is the boundless ocean, bellowing waves and fierce winds. This is a desolate corner for reflection and

Cabo de São Vicente

SIMON DANNHAUER/SHUTTERSTOCK ©

rambles. The headland is named after Spanish-born martyr São Vicente, who was torched alive by the Romans. The Portuguese version of the legend claims his remains were buried here before being exhumed and taken to Lisbon. Nearby **Fortaleza do Beliche** has long been closed due to erosion.

Around Sagres

Sagres is reportedly where Prince Henry the Navigator founded his legendary nautical school, used to drive early exploration and colonisation. However, most historians agree that the caravels sailed from Lagos; though records confirm he did build some kind of village-home here, the Vila do Infante, later in life. Contemporary low-rise Sagres remains equally ocean-focused, with surf schools, fish auctions, chilled-out bars and a handful of fantastic beaches. East-facing **Praia do Martinhal** is best for bathing, as it's more protected from the *Nortada* (west coast summer winds), while **Praia do Telheiro**, up the coast from the cape, is a hard-access secluded escape.

A CHURCH DETOUR

The combined ticket includes the small, 15th-century Ermida de Nossa Senhora de Guadalupe chapel, 20 minutes inland, though Vila do Bispo's (free) church is arguably more atmospheric.

Drive the Costa Vicentina

The Costa Vicentina is best experienced slowly, but those short on time can appreciate the park's historical highlights, varied landscapes and dramatic beaches on a whirlwind driving tour. Plan to be on the road from breakfast until sunset to visit all the attractions; allow extra time for detours to remote shorelines.

START	END	LENGTH
Burgau	Odeceixe	115km; 2½ hours

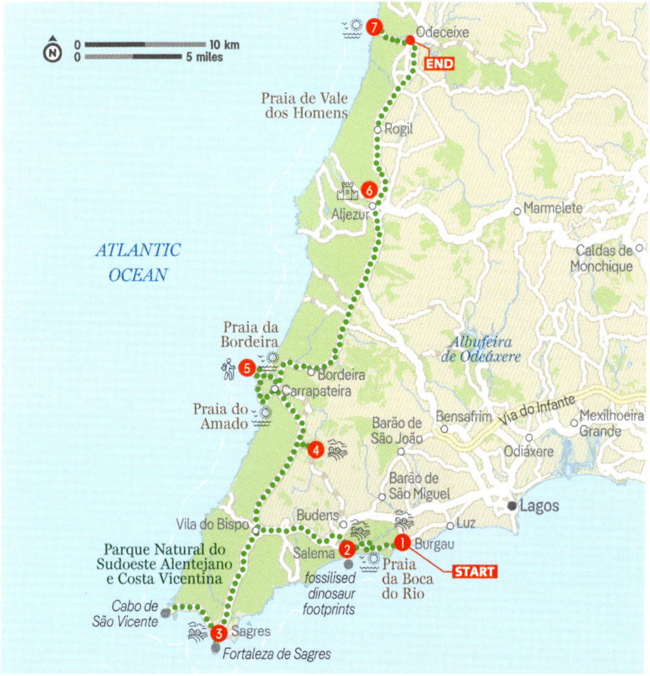

1 Beach Breakfast

Begin in **Burgau**, a cliff-flanked, whitewashed village marking the start of the Parque Natural do Sudoeste Alentejano e Costa Vicentina. After breakfast (**Os Amigos** has excellent pastries), stroll the narrow streets, admiring azure-lined doorways draped in bougainvillaea and the ocean views.

2 Fossilised Footprints

Relish the verdant scenes on the short drive towards **Salema**, taking a brief detour to **Praia da Boca do Rio**, a former Roman port. Enjoy your first paddle of the day in the crystal-clear waters before seeing **fossilised dinosaur footprints** near the western staircase.

3 Edge of Europe

Back on the main road, you'll soon reach **Sagres**. Plan to spend at least an hour here touring the imposing **Fortaleza de Sagres** before a brief drive to **Cabo de São Vicente**, a wind-ravaged headland and mainland Europe's most southwesterly point.

4 Whitewashed Village Lunch

Leaving the coast, it's around a 30-minute drive inland to **Aldeia da Pedralva**, a typically whitewashed Algarvian village that was once almost abandoned, but has been reborn as a diffused hotel. Reserve for lunch in the restaurant (noon to 2pm).

5 Scenic Detour

Before Carrapateira village, turn left towards ethereal **Praia do Amado**, backed by low-slung hills. Follow the **Pontal da Carrapateira Trail** by dirt track road, pausing at the Islamic ruins and viewpoints before stopping for a second swim at dune-backed **Praia da Bordeira**.

6 Moorish Memories

You can drive to Aljezur's **castle**, but it's better to park in town near the bridge. Ascend on foot, weaving through the Moorish quarter's web of narrow streets.

7 Sunset Swims

Set your sights on **Praia de Odeceixe**, the Algarve's final beach before the Alentejo regional border, for sunset. Here, the Ribeira de Seixe completes its journey from the Serra de Monchique, curving around the sand as a calmer swimming alternative. If you've time, detour to other beaches, such as **Praia da Amoreira**. At dusk, pop into **Odeceixe** village to grab dinner and see the **Moinho de Odeceixe windmill**.

EXPERIENCES

Catch a Wave

SURFING

The Costa's combination of serious surf sites and beginner-friendly bays makes it a wave-riding destination for all levels. Schools span the coast, with package prices dependent on the number of learning hours, gear rental and accommodation. Expect to pay around €60 for full-day group lessons. Sara and Celso run slick and long-standing **Sagres Natura Surf Camp** (MAP: 1 P144 A2; *sagresnatura.com*), providing an ideal learning base due to Sagres' west-facing beaches and more sheltered southern bays, while upcoast **Arrifana Surf School** (MAP: 2 P144 C3; *arrifanasurfschool.com*) teaches on the beach's sand breaks set against dramatic volcanic cliffs. The calmer waters between June and August are more beginner-suited, while the more challenging conditions between September and November (and throughout winter) will appeal to experienced surfers. Southern Praia do Zavial is a decent pick for easing in, while western Praia da Bordeira has two consistent breaks. Strike up a conversation at any beach bar, and you'll soon get some excellent recommendations from the local community.

Experience Atlantic Ocean Adrenaline

DIVING & COASTEERING

Adventurers aren't only spoiled with surf on the west coast – the fierce, shipwrecking Atlantic Ocean can be embraced in numerous ways. Sagres' **Divers Cape** (MAP: 3 P144 C8; *diverscape.net; prices vary*) provides PADI-certified courses and guided dives, including to the L'Ocean wreck sunk in the 1759 battle of Lagos, its skeleton and cannons now a flourishing artificial reef. Coasteering between caves and cliffs is best experienced around Raposeira's rock formations and overlooked grottos. Lagos-born Nelson, who knows the coast inside out, offers half-day tours at **Coastline Algarve** (MAP: 4 P144 C7; *coastlinealgarve.com from €55*).

Explore the Coast by Boat or Kayak

TOURS

Sagres-based **Mar Ilimitado** (MAP: 5 P144 C2; *marilimitado.com;*

BIRDWATCHING

During the winter and spring, the west coast – especially around Sagres – is soundtracked by migratory birdsong. Thousands of visitors (and seabirds) flock to **Sagres Bird Watching Festival** every October, where a packed four-day schedule of prebookable birding events forms Portugal's biggest nature-focused event. Throughout the park, you might spot griffon vultures, various buzzards, and Spanish imperial eagles. Rarer sightings include falcons and ospreys, who started to nest here again in 2014.

from €40) and its team of marine biologists and students double as a coastal research centre and a tour operator, offering dolphin, seabird and coastal sailings around Cabo de São Vicente. For a more active exploration, **South Kayaks** (MAP: 6 P144 **C7**; *southkayaks.com; from €30*) tours paddle away from Praia da Ingrina in search of calmer caves and goose-barnacle-clad rocks.

Find Your Perfect Beach BEACHES

From southern Burgau's village-backed bay to the wildest west coast cove, the Costa Vicentina's beaches are sublime. Dusty, gravel side roads lead to many often-empty pockets of sand, rewarding those with time to take the slow detours. Some of the standouts include the secluded sands of verdant cliff-wedged **Praia do Castelejo** (MAP: 7 P144 **B6**; drive first to the Miradouro da Cordoama for far-reaching panoramas) and walking across the cinematic rolling dunes of **Praia da Bordeira** (MAP: 8 P144 **C5**) to reach the vast remote-feeling shoreline. **Praia da Amoreira** (MAP: 9 P144 **D2**) is family-friendly, as the sandy estuary snakes far inland, providing calmer paddles and the occasional river otter sighting. The Algarve's most northern beach, **Praia de Odeceixe** (MAP: 10 P144 **D1**), is a show-stealer, with the scenic border-defining Rio Seixe calmly wrapping around the sand before meeting the ocean, making it an excellent SUP spot; board rentals are available from the beachfront surf school **Water Element** (see 10; *water-element.pt; from €25*). Hidden around the corner is the nudist beach of **Praia das Adegas** (MAP: 11 P144 **D1**).

Get a Bird's-Eye View PARAGLIDING

Soaring above swell and ocean-sculpted cliffs, the area's abundant birdlife gets to observe the coast's best panoramas. Why not join them on your first paragliding foray? World Cup competitor **Nelson Pacheco** (*flytripalgarve.webnode.pt; from €100*) offers introductory, 10- to 15-minute tandem paragliding experiences (and extended courses) around Praia da Cordoama.

Trace Carrapateira's Coastal Trail TRAIL

While not officially part of the Rota Vicentina (oddly, the route bypasses this scenic headland), the 11km circular **Pontal da Carrapateira Trail** (MAP: 12 P144 **C5**; *pontaldacarrapateira.com*) is one of the Algarve's best cultural and coastal routes. Starting at **Museu do Mar e da Terra da Carrapateira** (MAP: 13 P144 **C5**; *closed weekends*), a small but informative space with wide ocean-framing windows, the well-signed route is almost an open-air museum. Plan to spend at least half a day tracing the trails' giant, rusty metal letters denoting the main landmarks.

CREATIVE WORKSHOPS

From time-worn crafts to contemporary concerts, there are plenty of cultured ways to experience the Costa. At the pop-up, one-day workshops hosted by **Atelier Balancê** (*atelierbalance.net; prices and venues vary*), Ysaline teaches the ancient technique of palm weaving – the Algarve's dwarf palm tree is Europe's only native species – and upcycling basketry methods. If pottery is more your passion, book traditional clay-shaping classes at **Burros & Artes** (MAP: 14 P144 D3; *burrosartes.com; from €60*) hinterland farmhouse.

Highlights include dune-backed Praia da Bordeira, 12th-century Islamic fishing village ruins, and glimpses of those working the rugged rocks for *percebes* (goose barnacles) around Zimbreirinha's wooden fishing hut outpost, all with compelling coastal views. It's a fairly low-intensity clifftop trail, while bikes and cars (there are occasional parking spots) can follow the dirt-track road.

Amble with Donkeys

WILDLIFE SANCTUARY

Donkeys were once the Algarve's integral agricultural workers, but now, while some continue to drive carts and support farmers on the land, most have retired to sanctuaries. At **Burros & Artes** (*burrosartes.com; from €60*), a 10-minute drive northeast of Aljezur, you can accompany their well-cared-for furry friends on prebooked verdant valley walks. If you'd prefer a peek into working rural life, **ProactiveTur** (*proactivetur.pt*) arranges half-day working farm experiences in Rogil.

Step Back in Time

PREHISTORIC MONUMENTS

In this land, dinosaurs wandered, Neolithic people erected menhirs, and the Romans established fishing outposts – the remains of most still visible today. **Vila do Bispo Museum** (MAP: 15 P144 C7; museuviladobispo.pt; adult/child €5/€2.50), housed in the converted granaries of the Algarve's former bread basket, is the best jumping-off point for historical context. The contemporary space, opened in 2024, introduces the area's prehistoric sites, with megalithic stones and artefacts on display. Afterwards, drive towards the coast to see the easily accessed **Menhir do Padrão** (MAP: 16 P144 C7) before continuing to Praia da Salema's Early Cretaceous period **fossilised dinosaur footprints** (MAP: 17 P144 D7; best seen from the wooden stairway at the western end) and the Roman settlement of Boca do Rio – though most of the ruins are only visible underwater.

Explore Aljezur's Moorish Monuments

MUSEUMS & RUINS

The Moors' legacy lives on in Aljezur, its Arabic-derived name meaning 'the island' due to the rivers once surrounding the small Moorish town. Visit the weekday-only **Museu Municipal** (MAP: 18 P144 **D3**; *cm-aljezur.pt; €2.20*), where one room spotlights Moorish Aljezur, before climbing the steep, narrow streets flanked by whitewashed houses to the well-preserved walls of visitable 10th-century **Castelo** (MAP: 19 P144 **D3**). A short drive in either direction will bring you to more open-air Moorish ruins: the remains of **Ribat da Atalaia**'s Islamic fortress (MAP: 20 P144 **C3**) and the cliff-topping fishing village of **Povoado Islâmico de Pescadores** (MAP: 21 P144 **C5**). In November, the town holds a **Sweet Potato Festival** (*festival-batatadoce.cm-aljezur.pt*) honouring the potatoes that legends say formed the potion which aided the Christians in conquering Aljezur.

Visit a Reclaimed Rural Village

VILLAGE

MAP: 22 P144 **C6**

Inland from Vila do Bispo, the small, whitewashed village of **Aldeia da Pedralva** is one of the Algarve's greatest stories of recent revival. Once, a community of some 100 people lived here, but by 2006, the population had dwindled to just nine. A crowdfunding operation led to most of the abandoned homes being purchased, and over the following decade, a passionate team set out to restore the village. Many traditional timber-beamed homes became diffused hotels, complete with restored furnishings, and the old post office and communal oven were also returned to their original glory. Even if you're not staying overnight, it's a delightful spot to stop for lunch at the **traditional restaurant** (*noon to 2pm and 7pm to 10pm*), buy handicrafts from the artisanal market, hike on the Rota Vicentina, or hire mountain bikes to explore the interior.

PERCEBES

Percebes (goose barnacles) are the Costa Vicentina's most cherished crustaceans. Hand-harvested by death-defying *percebeiros*, who face fierce waters at daybreak to chisel the barnacles from ocean-ravaged rocky outposts, it's risky and time-consuming work that often sees the fishers diving underwater in aggressive waves. For this reason, they are rarely available in winter, when it's simply too dangerous to dive around the rocks. In June or September, Vila do Bispo's **Festival do Perceve** (*cm-viladobispo.pt*) celebrates the fearless fishers and their prized catch with a three-day event, including picking-method demonstrations and seafood feasts in barnacle-serving tents.

LISTINGS

Best Places for...

€ Budget €€ Midrange €€€ Top End

See p146 for map of locations

Eating

Sagres Seafood

A Sereia €€
23 C8
Atop the fish market with a window looking down at the catch arriving and afternoon auctions, seafood doesn't get fresher. *8am-5pm Mon-Fri*

Adega dos Arcos €€
24 B1
Expect worthwhile queues at this fisherman-run chargrill restaurant, where you can choose fresh fish from the counter. *noon-3pm & 7-10pm Tue-Sat*

A Tasca €€
25 C2
Grilled seafood and *cataplanas* against an ocean backdrop, while the stone wall and ceramic-decorated interior is snug on a windy day. *12.30-3pm & 6.30-9.30pm Thu-Tue*

Sagres Chic Spots

Three Little Birds €€
26 A2
Craft beers, home-baked bread, quality brunch, stacked burgers, and veggie options in a trendy surf-style bar and garden with summer live-music sessions. *10am-11pm Thu-Mon*

Bossa Brew House €€

27 B2
Microbrewery with an intriguing array of changing beers, a Portuguese and international menu, and occasional live-music jams. *noon-11pm Mon-Sat*

Laundry Lounge €€
28 A2
Wash your clothes while enjoying the trendy interiors, brunch, Asian menu and vegetarian options of this all-day hangout. *9am-11pm Tue-Sun*

Sagres Coffee & Sweet Treats

Picnic €
29 A1
Modern, small cafe with arabica bean barista coffee and a range of milk options. Cakes, bagels and other items are available for takeaway. *sunrise-sunset*

Alice Gelateria €

30 A2
Decadent hot chocolate, pastries and quality gelato make this the Costa Vicentina's go-to for sweet treats. *10am-9pm*

Burgau & Vale de Bispo Dining

Beach Bar Burgau €
31 D7
Right on the sand, with *palapas* (thatched shelters) for shade, the uninterrupted sea views elevate the seafood and snack menu. *10am-5pm Tue-Sun*

Ribeira do Poço €€

32 C7
Traditional Portuguese and seafood dishes, including barnacles and a fish counter, in an exposed-stonework interior in Vale de Bispo. *3-10pm Tue-Sun*

Carrapateira Eateries

Os Amigos da Carrapateira €
see 13
Unfussy, local and community-driven, this central cafe has a choice of breakfast pastries, snacks, and inexpensive daily specials. *9am-4pm*

Sítio do Forno €€

see 21
Clams and *cataplanas* are accompanied by clifftop views from the glass-protected external deck

restaurant near Praia do Amado. *noon-11pm Tue-Sun*

Aljezur Picks

Cervejaria Mar €€

 D3

Enjoy a seafood bonanza at this Aljezur hot spot particularly known for its *arroz de marisco* (seafood rice). *6-10pm Tue-Sun, from 12.30pm Sat & Sun*

O Sargo €€

 C3

The Japanese-fusion menu, paired with Praia de Monte Clérigo panoramas, makes this more than just another beach restaurant. *12.30-4pm & 6-9pm*

Moagem €€

see 

In Aljezur, this former mill house serves excellent vegetarian dishes with live music on Friday nights. *9.30am-4pm Sat & Sun, to 6pm Mon-Thu, to 2am Fri*

Odeceixe Favourites

Altinho €€

 D1

Climb the hill to this snug restaurant for friend-like service, seriously appetising sharing plates, and delicious dessert! *noon-2.30pm, 7-10pm Thu-Tue*

Ao Largo €€

 E1

Contemporary, airy interiors and tables spill out to the square with a healthy menu and vegetarian options. *8.30am-11pm Mon-Sat*

Drinking

Beach Bars

Castelejo

see 

Overhanging its cinematic namesake beach, this seasonal bar offers perfect cold-beer-sipping panoramas. *noon-7pm*

Esplanada do Mar

see 

Seconds from Odeceixe's sands, this seasonal snack bar has arguably one of the Algarve's best beach views to enjoy a coffee or fresh juice. *9am-8pm Wed-Mon*

Sebastião

 C7

Overlooking pretty Praia da Ingrina, this seasonal restaurant is a great place to grab an afternoon drink and watch wave-riding surfers. *11am-8pm*

Live Music

Salema Eco Camp

 D7

In summer, Salema's cool campsite is the place for starlit parties and performances by the likes of Raposeira Dub Collective. *hours vary*

Favo

 C7

Fun, friendly and trendy bar-restaurant in Raposeira pouring cocktails and craft beers with regular live bands and Wednesday salsa classes. *5pm-midnight Tue-Sat*

Shopping

Pottery

Ceramica Paraiso

see 

Plastered in colourful plates, this ceramic store is unmissable. There's a vast range of crockery and vases inside. *10am-6pm Mon-Sat*

Markets

Izzy's Market

 C7

Grab a coffee and shop packaging-free supplies in this cafe-cum-market specialising in sustainable items and organic produce, including locally produced, plant-based Acayú cheese. *10am-5pm Mon-Fri*

Mercado Municipal 25 de Abril

 A1

Sagres' farmers market is a great place for self-caterers to stock up on local produce, including prized Aljezur sweet potatoes. *8am-1pm Mon-Sat*

Algarve Toolkit

Praia da Bordeira (p153)
ADRIANA O./GETTY IMAGES ©

Family Travel

The Algarvian people's adoration for children is unmissable. Playgrounds are plentiful, breastfeeding is a non-issue, kid-friendly attractions are abundant, and even at evening cultural celebrations, children are a common sight. Family-friendly holidays here are breezy.

Getting Around

On trains and Vamus buses (store pushchairs underneath), children under three travel free and those aged four to 12 pay half the adult price. Pavements often aren't pram-friendly, especially as parking on them is common; consider packing a baby carrier or sling. Plenty of buggy-friendly boardwalks provide beach access and safe alternatives to unguarded clifftop trails.

ADULT TIME

Many resorts have kids' clubs and babysitters; some attractions provide similar. Albufeira's **Quinta do Canhoto** hosts painting classes while parents tour the vineyard, and at Portimão's **NoSoloÁgua**, adults can unwind as teens splash on slides.

Eating Out

Restaurants are generally very welcoming to kids, though baby-change facilities and *cadeiras de bebé* (highchairs) are less guaranteed. Some restaurants offer a dedicated *menu infantil* (children's menu), but if not, it's usually possible to order a *meia dose* (half-size portion) of most dishes. Evenings last longer here, and enjoying an after-dinner drink with kids on a bar's terrace isn't uncommon.

Attractions

Most waterparks offer advanced online discounts or family packages.

Many museums are free for toddlers and sometimes kids under 12.

NEIRFY/SHUTTERSTOCK ©

Zoomarine

This popular theme park near Albufeira has captive, performing dolphins; we recommend trying to see them **in the wild** instead.

Supervised Beaches

Many beaches have lifeguards from June to September, denoted by flags (p165). The eastern beaches are generally the calmest for paddling youngsters, especially the sands along the protected lagoon side of the Ria Formosa's islands.

Accommodation

With camping, hostels, *quintas* (farm or rural stays), family-run boutiques, affordable all-inclusives and even palaces, the Algarve has the lot.

Where to stay if you love...

Excellent eats and island beaches

Tavira (p55) The eastern Algarve's gateway has personality-rich accommodation and fair-priced, high-quality restaurants. An excellent car-free base with a calmer, 'authentic' atmosphere.

OUR PICK

We love to stay in...

Silves' Quintas (p115)

Stay at one of Silves' gorgeous boutique hotels or countryside ***quintas*** for a non-coastal break. The historic town packs culture, wineries and authentic restaurants without being overwhelmed by tourism. It's an excellent central base for the mountains and interior, while spectacular beaches are only a short drive, bus or train ride away.

Relaxed resorts close to the action

Galé & Salgados (p87) Albufeira's western resorts along sweeping Praia dos Salgados are far less loud and brash than around Oura, but only a 10-minute drive to downtown.

HOW MUCH FOR A HIGH-SEASON NIGHT IN

Basic guesthouse from **€50**

Boutique midrange hotel from **€120**

Luxury villa or resort from **€300**

Family-friendly coves and low-rise villages

Carvoeiro & Ferragudo (p101) Lagoa's two coastal villages have abundant self-catering accommodation rentals, laid-back nightlife, gorgeous sheltered beaches and nearby kid-friendly activities.

Beaches, nightlife and a varied crowd

Lagos (p129) Popular year-round for restaurants, bars, and accommodation. Activities and events abound. A reliable pick if you've little time for pre-trip research.

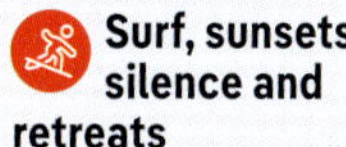

Surf, sunsets, silence and retreats

Costa Vicentina (p143) Sagres appeals to families, couples and surfers for laid-back vibes and walkable restaurants. Pick Pedralva or a farm stay for rural serenity.

Food, Drink & Nightlife

Allergies & Intolerances

Legally, establishments must provide allergen details for all dishes, though sometimes it's a separate, non-translated list. Always confirm if it's an *alergia* (allergy) or *intolerância* (intolerance). In Portuguese, 'no' means on/in, so 'no pão' means with bread, not without.

HOW TO SAY

I'm allergic to...	***Faço alergia a...***
nuts	***frutos secos***
peanuts	***amendoim***
seafood	***marisco***
dairy products	***lacticínios***
gluten	***gluten***

?

HOW TO ASK...

Is this gluten-free?
Isto é sem gluten?
Does this contain nuts?
Isto contem frutos secos?
Is there a vegan option?
Há alguma alternativa vegan?

COUVERT

Bread, olives, pâtés and cenoura à algarvia (marinated carrots) are usually served as couvert. It's a typical, unrequested yet paid-for appetiser, not a scam. Prices should be listed individually or combined (usually a couple of euros per person). If you don't want it (all or part), politely send it back.

Where to Eat When

Pequeno-almoço (breakfast, 7am to 10am) is usually a *tosta* or pastry.

Almoço (lunch, noon to 3pm) can be light at a snack bar or find a restaurante with a *menu do dia* (daily, fixed-price menu).

Jantar (dinner, 7pm to 10pm) is usually unhurried. Pick a restaurante, more-relaxed *tasca* (tavern), *marisqueira* (seafood restaurant), or *churrasqueira* (grill house).

Self Catering Scan this QR code for a Portugal shopping guide.

Pay the Bill

HOW TO...

Ask for the bill by saying, '*A conta, por favor*'. In general, it won't be brought to the table until requested. In some cafes, a prepayment system of ordering and paying at the counter (sometimes into a machine) is used.

Splitting the bill is usually done evenly. If paying by *dinheiro* (cash) rather than *cartão* (card), try to have smaller notes. Groups may be asked '*tudo junto*' (together) or '*separado*' (separate).

Tips aren't mandatory or automatically added. Some restaurants only accept tips in cash; say '*fique com o troco*' if you want the server to keep the change.

PRICE RANGES

The following price ranges refer to the average cost of a main course.

€ less than €12
€€ €12–25
€€€ more than €25

OPENING HOURS

***Pastelarias* (pastry shops/cafes) and *padarias* (bakeries)** 7.30am to 5pm

Snack bars 8am to 10pm

Restaurants noon to 3pm and 6pm to 10pm (most close one or two days per week)

DARYA LAVINSKAYA/SHUTTERSTOCK ©

Going Out

Sunset drinks are how many evenings start. Whether at an ocean-view cocktail bar or with a few bottles of beer or wine on the sand (public drinking is allowed).

Bars are abundant, from Irish pubs to trendy cocktail and wine bars or live music cultural associations. Snack bars double as laid-back evening drinking spots and are great to pair beers with some *petiscos* (small, sharing plates similar to Spanish tapas). Bars close between 2am and 4am, so there's no need to head to a club for a late drink.

Clubs don't tend to fill until after midnight, partying until at least 4am. Dress codes are generally relaxed; a few larger venues charge cover. Two of the biggest nightlife destinations are Praia da Rocha (more Portuguese) and Albufeira (more international). Some popular summer-only clubs, like **LICK**, are out of town. In summer, beach parties and even winery raves provide nightlife alternatives.

HOW MUCH FOR A

Café/bica (espresso) €0.85–1

Copo de vinho (glass of wine) €2–5

Imperial/caneca (small/large beer) €2/€4

Tosta mista (cheese and ham toastie) €3

Pastel de nata €1.50

Frango piri-piri (half) €7.50–10

Peixe grelhado (grilled fish) from €15

Cataplana de marisco (for two) €45

LGBTIQ+ Travellers

While the Algarve doesn't have many dedicated LGBTIQ+ venues, it's generally welcoming and accepting, especially along the more international coast.

Welcoming Spaces

Larger cities, including Albufeira, Faro and Portimão, have LGBTIQ+ venues, though you'll find unofficial queer-friendly spaces elsewhere.

Faro On Friday and Saturday nights, the fabulous Prestige Dance Club goes until 4am with drag shows, DJs and a welcoming local and international crowd.

Albufeira Start your night on the strip at Connection, a laid-back, first-floor terraced gay bar, before moving on to The Forest for drag or late-night dancing. Dark by Nude is a cruising venue.

Portimão Head to The Loft for a (sometimes themed) late-night party on Fridays and Saturdays. They also open on Tuesdays, but it's more chilled.

Nudist beaches Adegas in Odeceixe, Homen Nu in Tavira, and the western end of Ilha Deserta are designated official nudist beaches.

Accommodation

A double-bed request rarely raises an eyebrow, but expect more rural receptionists or hosts to reconfirm your request once or twice at check-in. Gay-only hotels include Casa Risa House & Spa (*casarisa.com*) inland from Alvor, which also offers massages and pool passes, and Lua Nua (*luanua.pt*), just across the Costa Vicentina's Alentejo border.

PRIDE

Faro has hosted the region's main pride parade every June for five years (*instagram.com/marchalgbtqialgarve*). A second, smaller event is usually scheduled for September in Lagos (*pridelagos.org*).

EVENTS

East Algarve Rainbow Club organises occasional LGBTIQ+ events, including drag and meet-ups, which are publicised on the GALAPT Facebook group.

Resources

- **ILGA Portugal Association** (*ilga-portugal.pt*) Portugal's main LGBTIQ+ association, based in Lisbon.
- **Proudly Portugal** (*proudlyportugal.pt*) The tourism board's LGBTIQ+ platform.
- **Rede Ex Aequo** (*rea.pt*) The main support group for 16- to 30-year-old LGBTIQ+ youth.

Health & Safe Travel

Low crime rates and few scams mean safety concerns are mostly related to the elements: sunburn, fires and ocean erosion.

WILDFIRES

Portugal is extremely prone to wildfires, especially Serra de Monchique. Drought and strong winds quickly turn small sparks into vast fires, relentlessly battled by mainly volunteer firefighters. Take care of cigarettes and barbecues. If hiking, check risk reports on *fogos.pt* or *ipma.pt* and carry lots of water.

Hospitals & Health Care

Portugal's National Health Service is complemented by usually bilingual private clinics. Local health centres (Centro de Saúde) handle prescriptions and non-emergency matters, often with long waits; call 808 242 424 (9 for English) for 24/7 non-emergency support and referrals. ERs (call 112) are in Faro, Portimão and Lagos. Ensure you have comprehensive health insurance alongside carrying reciprocal health cards, such as an EHIC or GHIC. Find local pharmacies (parapharmacies aren't for medication) on *farmaciasdeservico.net* (Faro District).

Theft

While uncommon, pickpocketing and car break-ins happen. The PSP, GNR or Municipal Police provide crime reports.

Erosion & Bathing

Pay attention to 'danger area' maps on cliff-backed and rock-overhanging beaches. When hiking atop cliffs, keep back from the edge; erosion poses a danger, and strong gusts and slips tragically lead to deaths annually. Lifeguarded beaches usually operate from June to September. Portuguese man o' war are extremely rare.

BEACH FLAGS

Seasonal lifeguard flags denote the bathing status: **green**, safe to swim; **yellow**, paddle close to the shore; **red**, danger/no swimming; **chequered**, temporarily unsupervised; **blue/purple**, dangerous marine life sighted.

QUICK INFO

Tap Water

Mains water is drinkable; some properties have boreholes.

Driving blood alcohol limit

0.5g/litre (0.2g/litre for drivers with a licence under three years).

Mosquitos

A summer annoyance: pack repellent.

Responsible Travel

In 2023, the Algarve welcomed more than ten times its population. Here are ways to help, rather than exacerbate, local issues.

Cultural Preservation

In recent years, the Iberian lynx and ospreys have been successfully reintroduced to the Algarve, providing a conservation win. However, with a heavily tourism-reliant economy, cultural preservation needs equal attention. Help keep traditions alive by sampling regional **traditional pastries and sweets** (p124) – the *toogoodtogo.com* app is excellent for trying an unexpected end-of-day batch – joining an ancestral techniques workshop with **Loulé Criativo** or attending folklore festivals.

Drought

The Algarve's drought situation is severe – and not only in summer. A campaign launched in 2024 asking travellers to reduce laundry, take short showers over baths, and not overfill swimming pools.

FROM LEFT:FRANK MCCLINTOCK/SHUTTERSTOCK ©, JULIA-ART/SHUTTERSTOCK ©

OUR PICK

Volunteer

Get active and involved on a **Rota Vicentina** maintenance hike *(rotavicentina.com)*. Locally organised beach cleanups and other projects are often published on *portugalresident.com*.

Coastal Conservation

The European Environment Agency ranked Faro as having Europe's third cleanest city air in 2024, only beaten by two Nordic cities. However, in summer, constant motorboats and car-clogged roads make a difference. Opting to cycle, kayak or snorkel to **lesser-trafficked sea caves** helps reduce pollution and protect marine ecosystems. If joining a boat tour, opt for a research project led by **marine biologists** (p160).

Resources

- **natural.pt** Details protected areas and parks
- **proactivetur.pt** Algarve ecotourism tour operator
- **quercus.pt** NGO focused on environmental issues

RECYCLING & REDUCTION

Deposit recycling at the many EcoPonto stations. Black is for general waste, green for glass, blue for paper, and yellow for plastic and metal. Packaging-free choices, such as **Izzy's Market**, and even in supermarkets, are expanding.

Seasonality & Spreading Out

While improving, seasonality has long been an issue for the Algarve's workforce in terms of contracts, income and housing. Planning a winter sun getaway or spring hiking trip supports additional year-round jobs while saving you money. Summer's soaring prices have also seen many Portuguese, who traditionally had family holidays in the Algarve, priced out. Checking self-catering accommodation is properly licensed – with an AL (*Alojamento Local*) number – helps somewhat combat housing supply, as does staying in lesser-visited or depopulating areas like the Eastern Algarve (p56) or interior villages.

CARAVANS & CAMPING

Restrictions control where and for how long overnight stays are allowed, including bans in natural parks and most coastal areas. **Scan the QR code to find official support areas and authorised parking zones.**

Climate Change & Travel

It's impossible to ignore the impact we have when travelling; Lonely Planet urges all travellers to engage with their travel carbon footprint, which will mainly come from air travel. While there often isn't an alternative, travellers can look to minimise the number of flights they take, opt for newer aircrafts and use cleaner ground transport, such as trains. One proposed solution—purchasing carbon offsets—unfortunately does not cancel out the impact of individual flights. While most destinations will depend on air travel for the foreseeable future, for now, pursuing ground-based travel where possible is the best course of action.

The **UN Carbon Offset Calculator** shows how flying impacts a household's emissions

The **ICAO's carbon emissions calculator** allows visitors to analyse the CO_2 generated by point-to-point journeys

Accessible Travel

Beaches

Around 45 Algarve beaches are designated accessible. In theory, the *praia acessível* flag should be flying near the accessible entrance point, and an access ramp and walkway are guaranteed. Some beaches also have adapted toilets or amphibious wheelchairs requestable from the seasonal lifeguard stations. See facilities on visitalgarve.pt.

Arrival & Transport

Book *MyWay* airport assistance at least 48 hours in advance with your airline. NGTours (*ngtours.com.pt*) offers accessible transfers; limited taxis are adapted. CP Trains' 'SIM support' is only offered for wheelchair users in the Algarve on Alfa Pendular trains to Lisbon (at Faro and Tunes); other mobility support is available at main staffed stations, bookable at least six hours ahead. Unlike regional public transport (p101), city bus networks have ramps and noise alerts on approach.

PAVEMENTS

Most city pavements are made from polished cobbles and are usually fairly flat, although often too narrow or parked over. Some curbs are dropped; tactile paving is limited. Find accessible walking tours (Faro, Lagos and Tavira) on visitportugal.com.

Portimão (p101) has been a regional accessibility leader since 2010, when it introduced the 6km Rota Acessível, forming the base of our **walking tour** (p106).

The **Museu de Portimão** has ramps, lifts, tactile flooring and an audio multimedia guide (via app or supplied device), including a VR experience to 'visit' the inaccessible cisterns. The city's accessible buses provide easy access to the marina area and beaches with boardwalks, including some with seasonal amphibious wheelchairs.

BOARDWALKS

An expanding network of passadiços (wooden boardwalks), including those in **Alvor**, **Carvoeiro**, **Faro**, **Lagos** and backing some beaches, provide (mostly) step-free access to birdwatching, viewpoints and shorelines.

Resources

- **TUR4all** (*tur4all.com*) has an expansive, collaborative database of sights and locations, including accessibility reports and photos, in multiple languages.

Nuts & Bolts

Opening Hours

Variations occur between cities and villages, and seasonally; in winter, unpublicised closures/reduced hours are common.

Banks/post offices 8.30am–3pm Monday to Friday

Bars 5pm–2/4am

Clubs 10pm–4am Thursday–Saturday

Markets 7am–2pm Monday–Friday

Museums 10am–1pm and 2–6pm Tuesday to Friday; weekend and Monday hours vary

Restaurants noon–3pm and 6–10pm

Supermarkets/malls 9am–10pm

Shops 10am–8pm Monday to Saturday, 10am–2pm Sunday

QUICK INFO

Time zone GMT/UTC (+1 during daylight saving)

Country code +351

Emergency number 112

Population 484,122 (The Algarve); 10.6 million (Portugal)

ELECTRICITY

230V/50Hz

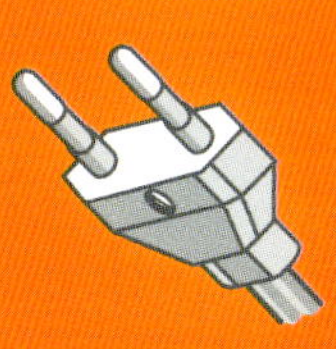

Drugs

In 2001, Portugal decriminalised the use and personal possession of drugs, making it a health issue rather than criminal. However, selling drugs, including marijuana, is illegal. While street sellers (often hawking poor-quality or fake products) are a rare annoyance, they can become aggressive when confronted; ignore them and walk past.

Public Holidays

On feriados (public holidays), banks and public services close, and public transport is extremely limited.

Dia de Ano Novo (New Year's Day) 1 January

Páscoa (Easter) March/April; Good Friday and Easter Sunday

Dia da Liberdade (Liberty Day) 25 April

Dia do Trabalhador (Labour Day) 1 May

Dia de Portugal (Portugal Day) 10 June

Assunção de Nossa Senhora (Assumption of Mary) 15 August

Implantação da República (Republic Day) 5 October

Dia de Todos os Santos (All Saints' Day) 1st November

Restauração da Independência (Independence Day) 1 December

Dia de Natal (Christmas Day) 25 December

Language

Basics

Hello.
Olá. *o·laa*

Goodbye.
Adeus. *a·de·oosh*

Please.
Por favor. *poor fa·vor*

Thank you.
Obrigado. *(m) o·bree·gaa·doo*
Obrigada. *(f) o·bree·gaa·da*

Excuse me.
Faz favor. *faash fa·vor*

Sorry.
Desculpe. *desh·kool·pe*

Yes./No.
Sim./Não. *seeng/nowng*

Fast phrases

Do you speak English?
Fala inglês? *faa·la eeng·glesh*

I don't understand.
Não entendo. *nowng eng·teng·doo*

A coffee
Um café *oong ka·fe*

Two beers
Dois cervejas *doysh ser·ve·zhash*

A table for two
Uma mesa para duas pessoas *oo·ma me·za pa·ra doo·ash pe·so·ash*

The bill, please.
A conta, por favor. *a kong·ta poor fa·vor*

How much is it?
Quanto custa? *kwang·too koosh·ta*

I'm a vegetarian.
Eu sou vegetariano/vegetariana. (m/f) *e·oo soh ve·zhe·a·ree·a·noo/ve·zhe·a·ree·a·na*

Where's ...?
Onde é ...? *ong·de e ...*

Where's the toilet?
Onde é a casa de banho? *ong·de e a kaa·za de ba·nyoo*

I'm just looking.
Estou só a ver. *shtoh so a ver*

Numbers

um *oong*

dois *doysh*

três *tresh*

quatro *kwaa·troo*

cinco *seeng·koo*

Good to know

Most sounds in Portuguese are also found in English. The exceptions are the nasal vowels (represented in our pronunciation guides by '*ng*' after the vowel), pronounced as if you're trying to make the sound through your nose; and the strongly rolled r (represented by '*rr*' in our pronunciation guides). Also note that the symbol '*zh*' sounds like the 's' in 'pleasure'. Keeping these few points in mind and reading the pronunciation guides as if they were English, you'll be understood just fine.

To enhance your trip with a phrasebook, visit *shop.lonelyplanet.com*. Lonely Planet iPhone phrasebooks are available through the Apple App store.

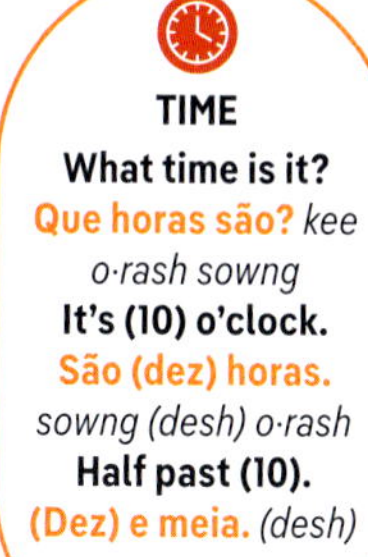

Emergenices

Socorro! Help!

Chame um médico! Call a doctor!

Chame a polícia! Call the police!

Estou doente. I'm sick.

Estou perdido/a. (m/f) I'm lost.

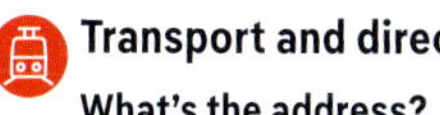

Transport and directions

What's the address?
Qual é o endereço? *kwaal e oo eng·de·re·soo*

Can you show me (on the map)?
Pode-me mostrar (no mapa)? *po·de·me moosh·traar (noo maa·pa)*

When's the next bus?
Quando é que sai o próximo autocarro? *kwang·doo e ke sai oo pro·see·moo ow·to·kaa·rroo*

I want to go to ...
Queria ir a ... *ke·ree·a eer a ...*

Does it stop at ...?
Pára em ...? *paa·ra eng ...*

Please stop here.
Por favor pare aqui. *poor fa·vor paa·re a·kee*

seis *saysh*

sete *se·te*

oito *oy·too*

nove *no·ve*

dez *desh*

TOOLKIT

Index

Sights **p000** Map pages p000

See also separate subindexes for:
Eating p174
Drinking p175
Shopping p175

Send Us Your Feedback

We love to hear from travellers – your comments help make our books better. We read every word, and we guarantee that your feedback goes straight to the authors. Visit lonelyplanet.com/contact to submit your updates and suggestions.

Note: We may edit, reproduce and incorporate your comments in Lonely Planet products such as guidebooks, websites and digital products, so let us know if you are happy to have your name acknowledged. For a copy of our privacy policy visit lonelyplanet.com/legal.

Acknowledgements

Cover photograph: Ponta da Piedade. Francesco Riccardo Iacomino/Getty images ©

Back photograph: Mosaic, Roman ruins of Milreu. trabantos/Shutterstock ©

THIS BOOK

Destination Editor
Annemarie McCarthy

Cartographer
Julie Sheridan

Production Editors
Megan Graieg, Alison Killilea

Book Designer
Catalina Aragón

Assisting Editors
Mani Ramaswamy

Cover Researcher
Lauren Egan

Thanks to
Fergal Condon, Gwen Cotter, Melanie Dankel, Soo Hamiton, Kate Mathews, Wayne Murphy, Charles Rawlings-Way

Published by Lonely Planet Global Limited

CRN 554153

3rd edition – Mar 2025

ISBN 978 1 78868 048 6

10 9 8 7 6 5 4 3 2 1

Printed in Malaysia